CYCLES of WAR

The next six years

by

R.E. McMaster, Jr.

For my children

Acknowledgments

To Jim Edmiston, President of the Bank of Columbia Falls, Montana, without whose provision for administrative back-up, this work would not have been possible.

To my wife, Linda, for providing me with a loving and tranquil home base which makes anything possible.

FOREWORD

It has become apparent from traveling around the country, speaking to investment groups and visiting with Americans, that there is a nagging sense of uneasiness about the future of the United States over the next few years. Investors are intent upon retrenching, maintaining their wealth. Caution is their watchword. The "sensitives" of the country - the psychics, poets, artists, composers, and writers - all express considerable insecurity over the future at hand. The intellectuals and educators are voicing concern. And the masses are beginning to feel impending danger. The nostalgia of the past few years is an indication of the wish to withdraw to more pleasant times. **Cycles of the War, The Next Six Years** brings to light the evidence that substantiates this national restlessness.

Contents

Chapter I

Introduction

" 'The institute of war lies close to the heart of mankind . . . In our recent Western history, war has been following war in an ascending order of intensity . . . If the series continues, the progression will indubitably be carried to even higher terms, until this process of intensifying the horrors of war is one day brought to an end by the self-annihilation of the war-making society' "[1]

This is the somber conclusion of the leading secular historian of the twentieth century, Mr. Arnold Toynbee. Toynbee's words are food for thought, particularly when one considers that Toynbee spent forty years writing three million words with well over 19,000 footnotes in his monumental work, **A Study of History.**

Yet, discussion of warfare among U.S. citizens is as rare as a fulfilled political promise. It could almost be classified as a social taboo, not proper for conversation at bridge clubs, cocktail parties, poker parties, or gatherings for Monday Night Football. It hardly goes down well with a Ritz or a Schlitz. Few Americans, however, would be willing to bet their life that the subject is unimportant. So, except for the poor souls plagued with hostile and/or destructive tendencies, war is a subject relegated to the movie makers, the military, the poets, and the philosophers - unlikely bedfellows to say the least.

Americans' exceptional aversion to warfare conversation has its roots in two fields. First of all, warfare and death are linked in the same harness. American culture's refusal to discuss death has been widely noted. Unlike the cultures of the Far East, which give consideration to the proper way to die, Americans skip across the field of life as though it goes on forever. Ever so often some poor soul slips into a hole. He is quickly covered, and those who follow scarcely notice that the newly filled hole ever existed.

But the sound of silence goes deeper than that. Americans are achievement conscious, success oriented, and gregarious. Warfare is stark social failure. It is the bottom line resolution of social problems unable to be solved in any other "civilized" manner. Paradoxical, isn't it? The aggressive American, subconscious and all, is reluctant to bring to the surface this most aggressive form of social failure.

At the outset, it is important to note that warfare doesn't spring upon one like a surprise party. One doesn't come home, unlock the door, turn on the light, and discover a war in the living room. Rather, it is like an approaching thunderstorm. The clouds build up, the darkness increases, and the thunder and lightning give advance warning. And like the typical reaction of those working outside during an oncoming storm, Americans assume the war will dissipate or detour around them, leaving them untouched.

For purpose of discussion here, warfare is to be considered any type of violent human conflict. **International warfare** is a social activity, requiring the greatest amount of teamwork and integration of effort by the whole society. Labor, the industrial complex, the military, the government - all subordinate their special interests to the violent adventure. Thus, international warfare necessarily take place between mature civilizations which are complex, technologically efficient, with sophisticated international communications, and pervasive government.

As Karl Von Clausewitz put it in his classic, **On War,**
> "*War is an act of force to compel our adversary to our will.*[2]

> It is . . . a continuation of policy by other means, the political intentions are the objects, and the war is the means. The nature of war is therefore determined by political objects . . . It is, therefore, a political act."[3]

Historically, the political act of war by the United States has "supposedly" been with the consent of the people.

While international war is an example of coordinated social process, the internal wars of the nation/state - revolutions, civil wars, riots - are a collapse of the social order, a disintegration of coordinated activity. Civil war occurs most often when there is a highly centralized government, if the nation is geographically large, and if the culture is heterogeneous. It can also be triggered by governmental failure to fulfill the expectations of ethnic groups, or when the necessities of life are in scarce supply.

Discussion of the causes of warfare falls within the boundaries of the evidence that focuses upon the timing factor. Timing in life is everything. Those who fish, make or catch passes, buy and sell stock, and fly airplanes will readily agree. If the weight of the evidence gives a high probability of warfare during a certain period of time, then one can ill afford to ignore structuring his activities accordingly.

It is the concern here that the nation will be forced to struggle with both internal conflict as well as international war within the next six years.

Chapter II

American Literature Cycles and War

Writers are members of that numerically insignificant group who reflect on the past and present, and sense the future. Accordingly, it should come as no surprise that the literature of a nation reflects its propensity for war.

Dr. David McClelland, professor of psychology at Harvard, has long had his finger on the pulse of American society, particularly as it relates to change. His research and study of the causes of human behavior has brought him widespread recognition. For example, in **The Achieving Society,** Dr. McClelland explored the relationship between the performance and personal need for achievement by people as a function of the average temperature where they and their ancestors had lived.

One of the more interesting, yet less publicized, studies made by Dr. McClelland was presented in the January 1975, **Psychology Today,** under the title of "Love and Power: The Psychological Signals of War." In this article, Dr. McClelland proposed a theory of the cause of warfare that has predictive value as well.

". . . the theory identifies certain motivational patterns that have typically preceded war by several years. When applied to the present, it seems to predict another American war in the near future.

. . . My data points strongly to this possibility. The American people are leaning more heavily

toward organized violence than at any time since 1825."[1]

Strong statements, to say the least. Dr. McClelland continued,

". . . the theory proposes that wars are a function of certain motivational patterns within a nation. The motives are the need for power (strength, authority, control over people and events) and the need for affiliation, or roughly, personal love - as both these motives are reflected in a country's popular literature . . . when the need for power is high,and higher than the need for affiliation, war tends to follow about 15 years later.

. . . The need for affiliation rises. Once it has risen as high as an already fairly high need for power, it then drops, leaving the need for power on top. A large-scale reform movement typically follows. The reform, in time, is followed by war.

. . . . Motivation seems to run before events."[2]

Dr. McClelland used three main sources of literature - children's texts, best selling novels, and hymns in testing his theory. The literary passages were coded for both the need for power, and the need for affiliation. The coders had no knowledge of the hypotheses and dates. The results were startling,

". . . out of 13 predictions extending through WWI, only one is incorrect. The decade of 1890 to 1900 is predicted to be peaceful, but in fact, the Spanish American War broke out in 1898. I doubt that this represents a serious flaw in the forecasting ability of the model, since the Spanish American War only lasted about 10 weeks . . . . Chance alone can hardly account for such accuracy."[3]

Using Dr. McClelland's theory, peace was correctly predicted from 1925-1935, and war from 1935-1945. A slight degree of affiliation over power caused an erroneous prediction for the Korean War.

It was Dr. McClelland's opinion that Vietnam was an exception to his predictive model. That makes sense. How could Vietnam be the result of the reform movement of the 1960's, since both occurred at the same time, and many of the reformers were unalterably opposed to the Vietnam War? Dr. McClelland believed that both Korea and Vietnam were the last gasps of the idealism that began in the 1930's. Vietnam was the death blow to old idealistic American hopes to serve as policeman for the world, and serve as the final arbiter of justice. It was further Dr. McClelland's view that the reform movement of the 1960's must yet result in a war. If the pattern repeats, the United States should find itself at war again some time in the late 1970's, maybe early 1980's. The violent action of the nation, self-righteous in nature, must be on the behalf of the poor, the down-trodden, and the oppressed. As the reform movement of the 1960's was one of the most staggering since the days of the Civil War, one might expect an aggressive and massive war effort in the future. Where could war break out? South Africa and the Middle East are two likely candidates. Dr. McClelland has a keen insight into war. He is a peaceful Quaker.

Dr. McClelland has raised a question for Americans. Do we have a President who is capable of leading (?) us to war, an idealist, maybe somewhat naive, who fits hand in glove with the nation's proclivity for war? The answer is so obvious it is scary. Georgia's vine-ripened Mr. Jimmy Carter fills the bin. A quick review of Mr. Carter's actions to date is appropriate: (1) The caretaker of his daughter - a convicted murderess, (2) The appointment of Andrew Young as U.N. ambassador with his subsequent global antics which have caused anger and embarrassment in Great Britain and South Africa, just to name two countries, (3) Mr. Carter's comments in the notorious **Playboy** interview, (4) His voluntary payment of $6,000 of income tax unnecessarily, (5) The imposing human rights issue which has alienated many countries, including the USSR. It is not farfetched to say that the "Wonder Woman" philosophy is alive and well in the White House.

Dr. McClelland comments,

"*. . . The personalities of reformers may be partly responsible. However altruistic and idealistic they are, their need for affiliation tends to remain low. We might call them lovers of mankind in the abstract rather than lovers of men and women. They are typically bent on the salvation of others regardless of anybody else's feelings in the matter. They tend, moreover, to be excellent organizers and managers, leaders and officers. This last point is crucial, for it suggests that certain idealistic individuals serve as actualizers or executors of a nation's motivational tendencies, translating sentiments into events. . . .*"[4]

Dr. McClelland's comments are a mirror image of Mr. Carter.

Dr. Billy Graham held an evangelistic campaign in the Carolina's in early 1977. His opening quotes from authorities citing the poor condition of planet Earth were designed, as usual, to scare the hell out of his audience. One of Dr. Graham's statements was particularly chilling. He quoted a Western European psychiatrist who felt we were due for a major war shortly. He stated that while on one hand people hate war, on the other hand they become bored for war. Dr. McClelland's work now has added predictive power.

Later, in October 1977, Jack Mabley, in his column, featured an article entitled, "A Worry or A Warning." Mabley noted that the United States ". . . had gotten out of several depressions and recessions by going to war. Democratic Presidents have presided at these wars."[5] He brought to his readers' attention the fact that Lloyd deMause, who edits the **Journal of Psychohistory**, concluded, ". . . the military overtones of the Carter imagery have delegated him to the role in which 'he is very likely to lead us into a new war by 1979.' "[6]

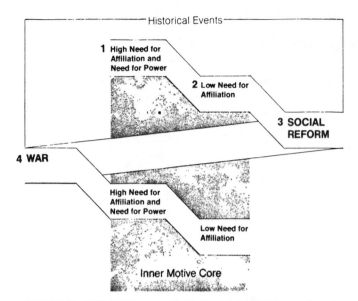

A TYPICAL CYCLE. When a nation's need for Affiliation and need for Power are both high (1) in a nation's popular literature, the need for Affiliation tends to drop (2). The resulting higher need for Power is often followed by some large-scale reform movement (3), which in turn appears to lead to war (4). Identifiable motivational patterns thus precede great public events.

WAR & PEACE IN AMERICAN HISTORY. From the founding of the Republic through World War I, the motivational pattern measured at the midpoint of any decade predicts that either war or peace will occur during the decade beginning 15 years later. The Spanish-American War is a notable exception to the model. After World War I, the lead time between motivations and events becomes much shorter. Despite this ambiguity, the militant "high" for 1965 seems to predict a war within the present decade.

Cont.

Source - Psychology Today - 1975[7]

Need for Power Greater Than Need for Affiliation (Gap)*	Lead Time	Social Reform		Lead Time	Actual War or Peace
1785 LOW					
1795 HIGH					1800
1805 HIGH		Jeffersonian Democracy			1810
1815 LOW					War of 1812
					1820
1825 HIGH					1830
1835 LOW		Jacksonian Populism			1840
1845 HIGH					Mexican War
					1850
1855 LOW		Abolitionism			1860
1865 LOW					Civil War
					1870
1875 LOW					1880
1885 LOW					1890
1895 HIGH					Spanish-American War
					1900
1905 LOW		Crusade for Social Justice			1910
1915 (NO DATA)					World War I
					1920
1925 LOW					1930
1935 HIGH		New Deal			1940
1945 LOW					World War II
					1950
1955 LOW					Korean War
					1960
1965 HIGH		Civil Rights			Vietnam War 1970
					War?
					1980

*When need for Affiliation is actually greater than need for Power, the gap is considered "low."

Chapter III

Cycles of Monetary Instability and Civil War

The prospect of a second American Revolution was discussed in the November 1976 issue of **International Moneyline** when Crane Brinton's, **Anatomy of Revolution** was reviewed. Brinton had studied the periods of time just prior to four major revolutions. He analyzed the French Revolution, the Russian Revolution of 1917, the American Revolution, and the Glorious Revolution of England in 1642. The similarities of these periods with present conditions in the United States are ominous.

He found that in each situation, revolution was foreshadowed by the potential or actual approaching bankruptcy of the government. It is not with much comfort that we note that the National Tax Foundation has reported the commitments and liabilities of the U.S. Government to be in excess of $7.56 trillion currently.[1] The words of Thomas Jefferson return to haunt us. "I place economy among the first and most important virtues, and public debt as the greatest of dangers . . ."[2]

Just as serious a threat today is inflation. Inflation is simply the result of an increase in the supply of money. And since government is creator of money, and regulates the supply thereof, it is the author and finisher of the inflationary work. Amen. The government can work to increase the money supply through the Federal Reserve's open market operations, the discount rate, and reserve requirements, through the fractional reserve banking system which creates credit, or simply by printing money. The editor of **The London Times,** William Ress-Mogg, wrote a timely volume entitled, **The Crisis of World Inflation.** In it he noted,

> "Ruin and revolution are the normal consequences of inflation . . . . [3]
>
> There is no inflation which has not started with an increase in the money supply; there is no inflation which has not ended with a corruption of society, proportionate only to the degree of the inflation itself. It corrupts and weakens every social institution; it makes every member of society feel himself to be the victim of every other member of society; it sets class against class. It makes governments weak and unsure of themselves; it has in recent history destroyed more lawfully consituted governments than any other force except war itself.
>
> This is because all inflation is by its nature both inordinate and unjust; in the end it destroys wealth, but from the start it makes a great transfer of wealth, both between classes and inside classes, which does not reflect work or merit or economic contribution, but skill in speculation, luck, militancy or industrial bargaining power. It makes the whole economic system seem unjust and the whole political system seem ineffective. It makes men take short views; when money is good men plant oaks, when it is bad they can at best plant cabbages. It makes men corrupt, both by impoverishing them arbitrarily and by enriching them arbitrarily."[4]

The good editor notes other "benefits" of inflation. It is very unjust to women; it causes the poor to suffer most; it does the work of Marxism; it causes insecurity which turns the population toward political extremists, usually a Caesar type.

Along the same line, the 1974 Nobel Prize winner in Economics, F.A. Hayek, stated in an article in the August 19, 1977, issue of the **Wall Street Journal,**

"I have always defended the gold standard, and later fixed exchange rates, not because I thought they resulted in particularly good money but because they provided the only effective protection from government abuse of its monopoly to issue money.

But now, when this discipline has broken down, I see no hope of its being ever restored.

Therefore, unless we fundamentally change things, our prospect seems for indefinite accelerating inflation worsened by price controls, followed by a rapid breakdown of the market, of democratic institutions and ultimately of civilization as we know it."[5]

Brinton pointed out some other conditions which can precede revolutions, which **International Moneyline** noted,

"All major revolutions witnessed:

1. A long period of economic growth followed by a period of sluggish growth, or decline.

2. The frustration of rising expectations of the middle class and lower class, who had become used to getting a little more every year.

3. A ruling class divided and inept with many feeling guilty about their position or being overly sympathetic to the social and economic underdogs.

4. A significant increase in corruption, crime, and general immorality.

5. Increased rebelliousness and alienation of youth from the older generation.

6. *Desertion of the establishment by the intellectuals and increasingly harsh attacks and criticism.*

7. *Abdication of the electorate . . . that is, increased indifference to politics on the part of the general population, making it possible for small, tightly organized groups to wield influence, or to take over . . ."*[6]

The United States scores highly on points 1, 2, 3, 4, 5, and 7. The clock is running, and so the key is one of timing. Enter L. J. Jensen.

Mr. L.J. Jensen is a student of markets, a scientist, and an astral observer. He is a wise man. There are few like him. Historically he is most like the Magi, the Zoroastrian priests of ancient Media and Persia who came from the East to find Jesus. In 1935, Mr. Jensen wrote concerning the upcoming 1980 period,

> *"In checking economic statistics of the business cycle with the periods when the major slow moving planets, Saturn, Uranus, and Jupiter, are ninety or one hundred eighty degrees apart in the zodiac, they are found to coincide with economic depression . . . .*
>
> *The earth signs of the zodiac, Taurus, Virgo and Capricorn, have always been closely coupled to American political and financial life. The passage of planets through these signs in their revolutions tie in with major events in a startling manner. For the first time in the United States history, Jupiter and Saturn began to meet in conjunction in earth signs just after 1840. Regularly every twenty years since a conjunction of these two planets has occurred in these earth signs, timing periods of political upheaval and new agitation, and interest; - in currency, national credit and financial matters."*[7]

Mr. Jensen also noted in **1935** that since the beginning

of these conjunctions in earth signs, every President who was elected in these periods died in office.

1840 - Harrison, 1860 - Lincoln, 1880 - Garfield, 1900 - McKinley, 1920 - Harding, 1940 - Roosevelt, 1960 - Kennedy, 1980 - ?

Mr. Jensen must be taken seriously. Also, in 1935, he wrote that 1943-44 would be "the most momentous period so far encountered in American history."[8] His work has now been confirmed by Lieutenant-Commander David Williams, USN, Ret., in the 1970's. Mr. Williams has discovered that the human nervous system, including the brain, works by means of tiny electric impulses. Changes in solar radiation, changes in the earth's magnetic environment, cause subtle changes in the electronics of the human mind and body. There are periods when, as a result of these changes, people tend to get irritable, jumpy, pessimistic, and make poor judgments. Mr. Williams checked his economic history back to the 1700's. He found that certain planetary positions coincided with the changes in solar radiation and the earth's magnetic environment which further dovetailed with economic booms and busts. He found that major long-term economic cycles corresponded with the movements of Saturn, Uranus, and Jupiter.[9]

In the January 1977 issue of **Cycles**, Jack Sauers, a geologist and member of the Foundation for the Study of Cycles, added to the evidence,

"... *only every other 50-year cycle does the U.S. solve its monetary problems by going back on the gold standard. Perhaps you can add your current Federal Reserve Notes to your collection of Civil War greenbacks and Confederate money of 100 years ago or your Continentals, the Revolutionary script of 200 years ago ...*"[10]

The gold bugs should smile. We should return shortly

to a gold standard. Unfortunately, if Sauers' cycle occurs, we will have a revolution to live through first.

Chapter IV

Planets, Cycles, Climate, and War

Very small changes in climate cause severe disruptions in the affairs of men. After exhaustive research this conclusion was reached by Nels Winkless III and Iben Browning in their scholarly work, **Climate and the Affairs of Men.** Their study revealed that,

"Changing climate alters the amount and nature of food supply . . . the marginal croplands of the world become submarginal and food production even in comparatively rich agricultural areas is disrupted. . . highly productive food plant strains cannot tolerate large variation in environment . . . .

War, migration, economic upset, and changing ethics mark hard times."[1]

This situation is accentuated in a cooling trend such as we are facing presently. **The Morgan Guaranty Survey** of New York, March 1977, noted that 23 of the 28 scholars who published papers on climatology in recent years thought the earth will be cooler within the next decade than it is today.[2]

Winkless and Browning concluded that the affairs of men were dictated by the release of energy that had been stored in the earth (earthquakes and volcanoes), and that this energy release was triggered by extraterrestrial forces. They noted that the climate in the recent past has been the warmest and most benevolent in hundreds of years, and the world should return to more "normal" conditions,

conditions far more harsh.[3] With regard to the effect of these changes on the United States, they remark, "The times of great temperature change, therefore times of great variability, are marked by combativeness among the residents of the United States. That great dip in things marks the time of the Civil War. . ."[4]

Cyclical research revealed that over the next five years, in addition to being a time of great change, characterized by average lower temperature, the earth should also experience drier conditions and great climatic variability.

They noted that the 800-year cycle in the affairs of men is here. The 800-year cycle has been documented seven times. Each time the cycle has been characterized by historic migrations, drought, famine, and warfare.[5] C.G. Abbot, retired Secretary of the Smithsonian Institute, believes that the 45-year cycle is here also. That cycle has marked painful events like the depression of 1838, the agricultural problems of 1886, and the Great Depression of the 1930's.[6]

Winkless and Browning have established their credibility. Their book, written in the early 1970's, predicted,

"The next two or three years - 1975, 1976, and perhaps 1977 - should provide relief to the planners and organizers around the world . . . .

Drought should plague the U.S. western Great Plains and Canada (says Abbot), and if the traditional pattern holds, we'll have a depression. The world will heave a sigh of relief that the times of strange weather are coming to an end and we're getting back to normal. Average temperature will still be low, but the patterns will seem familiar.

Alas, the climatic respite ends, the patterns will shift again and the illusion will be shattered."[7]

Let's see. As predicted, relief to world planners came in 1976 and 1977 by way of record food crops. The drought is in evidence in the western U.S. and Canada. The U.S. experienced a severe recession in 1974 and 1975, and the world a slight depression during the same period. When will the present climatic respite end? If Winkless and Browning are to be believed, the fat will hit the fan and cause severe problems from 1978 forward.

Mr. Edward R. Dewey, in his book, **Cycles, The Mysterious Forces That Trigger Events,** discussed the work of the late Professor Raymond H. Wheeler of the University of Kansas. Dr. Wheeler compiled 2500 years of records in 20 years employing some 200 people. Dr. Wheeler felt that the most important climatic cycle in the affairs of men was the 100-year cycle. He too felt that climate/weather and human action were closely related. He noted that the 100-year cycle could contract to 70 years or extend to 120 years.[8]

The 100-year cycle is divided into 4 phases which describe world conditions in general rather than for a specific area. The four phases are labeled: (1) Cold-Dry, (2) Warm-Wet, (3) Warm-Dry, and (4) Cold-Wet. In 1949, Dr. Wheeler thought the world would next be entering the Cold-Dry phase.[9] Undoubtedly, this is the world's climatic condition now. The characteristics of the Cold-Dry period are:

". . . *general individualism, with weak governments, migrations, and other mob actions such as race riots. Class struggles, and civil wars ranging from palace intrigues to revolutions occur during the general anarchy of the Cold-Dry period. People are cosmopolitan and Epicurean, borrowing culture and living by superficial and skeptical philosophies.*"[10]

One of the most astonishing accomplishments of Dr. Wheeler is depicted - a Drought and Civil War clock, taken from Ellsworth Huntington's (former Yale professor) **Mainsprings of Civilization**. Notice the dates in years around the outer edges of the clock. Immediately inside the edge is the 170-year Civil War Cycle. The three arcs in the interior represent the 510-year Civil War Cycle that coincides with drought. Notice that the intersection of the 170-year and the 510-year cycle next occurs around 1980.[11]

Mr. Dewey, who heads the Foundation for the Study of Cycles, has done his own research on war as well. With regard to the 142-year cycle in war, he states, "The 142-year pattern calls for a more than average number of battles for the seventy-one year period from 1914 to 1985 . . ."[12] Comments on the 57-year cycle in war in 1951 include, ". . . prudent men could not ignore the possibility that the next twenty-five or thirty years would see an increasing number of international battles."[13] Dewey also felt that the 1960's would be turbulent, and the middle 1970's "reasonably peaceful." He was right on both counts.

Mr. Dewey and the Foundation for the Study of Cycles, in their research of Dr. Wheeler's work, discovered four recurring cyclical patterns in the Index of International Battles. The synthesis of the four cycles (142-year, 57-year, 22.14-year, and 11.2-year) corresponded very closely to actual international warfare. The next most likely time for international war is 1982, when the combined cycles peak.[14]

Trouble comes in bushel baskets. The year 1982 is also the date of the major grand planetary alignment which John R. Gribben and Stephen H. Plagemann, both astrophysicists, postulated would trigger major earthquake activity. Their work was popularized in their book, **The Jupiter Effect**. Their thesis that the gravitational forces caused by the geocentric planetary alignment would

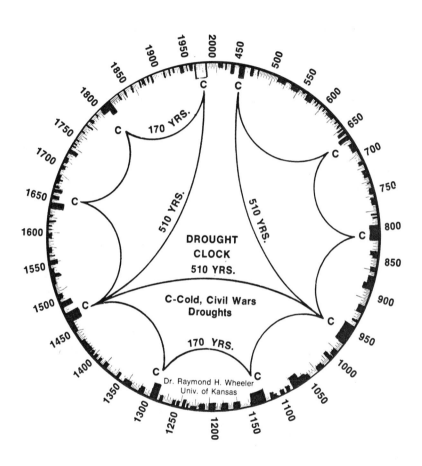

Source - Mainsprings of Civilization - 1945

touch off earthquakes was confirmed by Winkless and Browning. But it was also verified by Mr. John R. Nelson, formerly with RCA and a consultant to NASA and Jet Propulsion Laboratories.[15] As cycles stretch and shrink where humans are concerned, it is interesting to note that the grand alignment occurs only once every 179 years, and Dr. Huntington's 170-year Drought and Civil War Cycle coordinates within 5%.

Sunspot activity also deserves some attention. The year 1982 is the peak of the 11-year sunspot cycle. Sunspots alter the rate of the earth's rotation through interactions of the solar winds with the earth's magnetic field and atmosphere, which in turn sets up strains within the earth which results in earthquakes and volcanic eruptions.

Professor A.L. Tchijevski of the University of Moscow presented a paper to the American Meteorological Society in Philadelphia in 1926 which outlined an index of mass human excitability which correlated with the 11-year sunspot cycle.

"The maximum of human activities in correlation with the maximum of sunspot activity, expresses itself in the following:

a. *The dissemination of different doctrines (political, religious, etc.), the spreading of heresies, religious riots, pilgrimages, etc.*

b. *The appearance of social, military, and religious leaders, reformers, etc.*

c. *The formation of political, military, and religious and commercial corporations, associations, unions, leagues, sects, companies, etc."*[16]

He additionally noted that diptheria, cholera, typhus, smallpox, and influenza reached peak proportions during maximum sunspot activity.[17]

Our sun has been going through a hyperactive stage recently. The components of our sun, from outside to inner core, are hydrogen, helium, silicon, and iron (core). Astronomers have concluded that when the iron nucleus of a sun begins to break down into helium, overturning the balance between hydrogen and helium, the end of the life of that sun is approaching. It, the sun, or star, can do two things. It can explode (super nova), or simply nova. In either case, it means the end of life on this earth.[18]

The key to the life of the sun/star is hydrogen. Stars all over the universe are reaching nova or super nova once 51% of their hydrogen has been burned up. When 50% of a star's hydrogen content is gone, drastic changes begin to occur. Our sun has used up 50% of its hydrogen. Scientists project the life of our sun to between 10 years and ten billion years. Pretty broad parameters! But remember, 90% of man's knowledge about the heavens has been garnered since 1955.[19]

Professor of physics at the U. of Colorado, Dr. George Bamow, has stated that, in his judgment, from the sun's dramatic eruptions and resulting changes in weather, we may be facing an imminent decline in the energy produced by the sun. We should expect an increase in flares, magnetic storms, and huge sunspots. The increased gravitational pull upon the sun brought about by the grand alignment of planets (Jupiter effect) could produce solar storms to an extent never before known on our sun. Solar storms, of course, can trigger earthquakes and alter weather patterns.[20]

All this vibration could result in a polar shift. In such a case, the earth alters its axis and its center of gravity. When this occurs the earth's climate changes, the cold arctic regions become warm, mountains are lost under the seas, and the seas become dry. Concerning natural catastrophies the **Bible** states that when the ". . . sign of the Son of Man

is in the heavens, these things shall come to pass."
"Aquarius is the sign of the Son of Man."[21] Historically,
"On January 19, 1881, the sun passed from the water sign
Pisces into the air sign Aquarius, thus beginning a new cy-
cle of solar force."[22]

Mr. Robert H. Olsen had a few words to say about the
polar cap. He notes that an electrical engineer named
Hugh A. Brown of Long Island, N.Y., has been gathering
information for years on the ice cap at the south pole.
Brown calls it " 'man's glistening executioner.' " He estimates the growth rate of the Antarctic ice cap to be five
trillion tons per year. He believes, " 'One day the earth will
shiver and careen on its side, tipping over like a giant
overloaded canoe.' "[23] Twenty-six years after Admiral
Byrd planted 70 foot radio antennae on "Little America"
in Antarctica, members of Operation Deep-Freeze could
only find less than five feet of antennae above the icy surface. Ice on Antarctica is increasing at the rate of four
billion tons a day.[24] Could the Jupiter effect set off this
polar shift? Possibly so.

We already have signs of impending danger. The
strength of the van Allen belts and the Earth's magnetic
fields have been reduced. "The protective magnetic umbrella that shields the surface of the Earth from the
blasting plasma and ultraviolet rays from the sun is
diminishing more rapidly each year."[25] The earth's rotation has also started to slow ". . . as a portion of its enormous kinetic energy is used to resist the thrust of the polar
ice cap."[26] Clocks have been set back. We have seen world
wide heat waves. If and when we witness mutations in all
living things and increasing static, distortion, and drift of
radio waves, along with other interference with long dis-
tance communications, we will know that the time is at
hand.[27]

Additional research on the polar cap has been done by

James D. Hay of Columbia University, Nicholas J.
Shakleton of Cambridge University, and John Imbrie of
Brown University. These three scientists are members of
the CLIMAP project (Climate: Long-Range Investigation
Mapping and Prediction). Their work was reported in
Science, December 10, 1976, and was entitled, "Variations
in the Earth's Orbit: Pacemaker of the Ice Ages". As a
result of their extensive research, they concluded that, "...
present conditions are leading slowly toward colder
climate, as longer distances between the earth and the sun
in the summer result in cooler summer temperatures, with
less snow melting and subsequent growth of the polar ice
cap."[28] They also confirmed the earlier discussion that the
earth presently is as warm as it has been "... only 10% of
the time during the past million years, and climate is now
moving on the downside of the present warm period."[29]
When climate becomes brutal, the natives become restless
and aggressive.

The famous psychic, Edgar Cayce, said,

" 'Toward the very end of this century there will
be upheavals in the Arctic and in the Antarctic that
will bring the eruption of volcanos and earthquakes,
and there will be a shifting then of the poles - so that
where there have been those frigid or semi-tropical
will become the more tropical, and moss and fern will
grow.' "[30]

Whether or not there will be a nova of our sun shortly,
whether or not there will be a polar shift, is wide open to
question. Actually, there is little reason to guess.
Realistically, all that need be done is to sit tight, observe,
and gather the evidence. We know what to look for. What
is important is that during this type of disruption, or any
other type of change, mankind is unlikely to take it all in
calmly. Men resist change, particularly change that comes

as a surprise. One of his classic responses to unexpected change is violent action. Man's propensity for violence is the concern here.

Chapter V

Market Cycles and War

Markets and warfare are both social phenomena, and are energized by mass emotion and psychology. Thus, in doing research, it came as no surprise to note the great similarity between the two.

Let's look first at a market in the process of topping out. When sugar was barreling up in 1974, the cry was for the government to do something, for sugar was going to $1.00 it was said. Sugar at $1.00 would financially kill heavy commercial users. The housewife called for price controls. The overwhelming consensus was, "Sugar is going out of sight." Then, amid all the concern and panic, the sugar market started down, and in 1977 is selling below the cost of production. In this free market, price rationed the resource (sugar), until supply (production) could catch up. As price went up, marginal users were forced out of the market - a very natural and just allocating process. (This is found in the natural order. Where there are too many rabbits putting a strain on the grass, the coyote population increases until the rabbit population declines and the grass recovers.) The market tops out by demand being rationed by higher price, or by supply coming in, in excess of demand, or some of both.

When the government comes in and interferes with the market by slapping on price controls, it distorts the natural process. Shortages result as marginal users compete with those who really need the resource and would bid it higher.

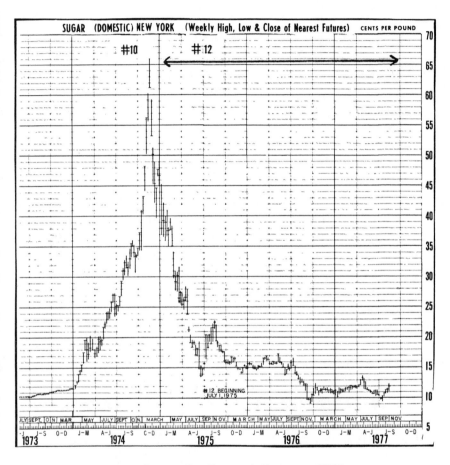

SUGAR (DOMESTIC) NEW YORK (Weekly High, Low & Close of Nearest Futures) CENTS PER POUND

Source - Commodity Research Bureau - 1977[1]

This autocratic involvement by government can lead to hostility among frustrated bidders while suppliers/producers of the resource do not have the increased incentive of higher prices to produce more. The same thing is true on the larger scale of international free trade. When government interferes through tariffs, embargoes, import quotas, and the like, it runs the risk of war in addition to economic distortion.

As Professor Ludwig von Mises, Dean of the Austrian School of Economics and teacher of Nobel Prize winner, F.A. von Hayek, stated in his masterpiece, **Human Action,**

> *"Under laissez faire peaceful co-existence of a multitude of sovereign nations is possible. Under government control of business it is impossible . . .*[2]
>
> . . . . *Economic nationalism, the necessary complement of domestic interventionism, hurts the interests of foreign peoples and thus creates international conflict."*[3]

As the world's population continues to increase, international unemployment is also increasing. The population demands that the government "do something" about unemployment. Government's expected scapegoat is foreign labor and products. Also, the world's population growth (85 million new folks annually) is running head-on into a major basic resource crisis (food, energy, water) in the early 1980's. Dewey's comments on international battles are particularly noteworthy,

> *"International battles clearly have their counterparts in both biological and economic cycles. By a 'biological' cycle I mean one that expresses itself predominantly in biological phenomena, such as animal abundance. By an 'economic' cycle I mean one that expresses itself predominantly in economic phenomena, such as prices and production. It is rare*

indeed for a phenomenon to evidence both kinds of cycles, but war does."[4]

Some quick comments on the basics of life - water, food, and energy - are appropriate.

WATER - Drinking water is inadequate in many parts of the world. Even the United States faces this crisis, long a European problem. In April of 1975, in Washington D.C., the largest conference ever organized on water was held, sponsored by the U.S. Water Resources Council, chaired by then Interior Secretary, Rogers C.B. Morton. It was concluded that unless there are changes in national policy, " '. . . the next generation may well face a water crisis of even greater consequence than our current energy situation.' "[5] There is danger that the entire area between Boston and Norfolk will go dry unless water sources are found. Lack of water leads to warfare. Remember the cattlemen's range wars in the 1800's over water rights? Historically, when a society starts to ration water, it is already streaking downhill.

FOOD - Water is necessary for food production. Former Agriculture Secretary, Earl L. Butz, warned that how water is utilized will determine how well the world will be fed as the population doubles to 8 billion in the next 35 years.[6] What if unfavorable weather returns as climatologists predict? (The armadillos are headed south!) Will there be a rerun of the 1973-74 food crisis, this time involving more people? What is to be done about the fact that 42% of the food produced in the world is lost to pests and rats according to Dr. David Pimintel of Cornell University and Dr. Ray F. Smith of the University of California in a talk given before the American Association of the Advancement of Science in 1977 ·in Denver, Colorado? The problem is compounded by the fact that pests are developing an increasing immunity to pesticides while the pesticides are destroying the predators and parasites that are the natural enemies of the pests. Catch 22! The amount of pesticide utilized today amounts to more than a pound per year for every person on earth and is increasing yearly. Some 90% of the eggs and larvae of crop pests would be destroyed by natural enemies, if the natural enemies could survive the pesticides.[7]

The food production problems are complicated by the fact that farmers, facing increasing costs and huge debts, are technically bankrupt with grain prices at pre-inflationary levels. The Production Credit Association and the local banks are all that stand between primary producers and ruin. Agriculture is a pillar of the American economy. Ironically, almost the same situation existed a century ago, prior to a depression.

The 219-page report by former President Ford's National Research Council Committee on food problems linked the basic causes of hunger with overpopulation and the need for the poor countries to produce more food. It noted that, " 'science and technology alone cannot improve the world's food and nutrition situation.' "[8] Government policies (interference in the market place) come into play. The earth's human population is increasing by 85-90 million a year, and as Dr. Reid Bryson, Director of the University of Wisconsin's Institute for Environmental Research, put it, "It really wouldn't take a very large shift in global weather patterns right now to make a year's harvest come up 25% short of the world's food demands."[9] Bryson has argued that giving away food aggravates the dilemma, for it leads to increased human reproduction. Bryson has also commented that the green revolution is a pipe dream. It has been underway for 20 years with no realized gain, and the cost of bringing to production the marginal acreage of the earth would run $1,000.00 to $2,500.00 per acre and this would only feed one person a year.[10] The problem is compounded.

Drought could consume one-third of today's arable land within the next 25 years.[11]

Dr. Raymond Ewell, fertilizer expert at State University of New York, stated that the world's food crisis is ' "the biggest, most nearly insolvable problem that has ever faced the human race.' "[12]

ENERGY - The Arab Oil Embargo of 1973 and the harsh winter of 1976-77 jolted the U.S. into the reality of an energy crisis. In 1977, the United States is importing 34% more foreign oil than in 1973. (Agriculture is now energy intense.) As C.V. Myers of **Myers' Finance and Energy** observed,

"1. We are using 73 quad. [A quad is a unit of oil, and is equivalent to what the U.S. was short in the 1973 oil embargo. Being short one quad crippled the U.S. economy.] 2. Normal growth under the very best technology will require a minimum 170 quad. 3. Absolute maximum conservation could only reduce this to 105 quad by yr. 2000. 4. Oil and natural gas are declining. 5. This will leave a gap of 26 quad which can only be filled by coal. 6. Calls for coal production of 40 quad compared to 15 quad today. 7. Capital requirements to reach minimum objective on all fronts will probably exceed a trillion dollars."[13]

Myers asked,

"How do we get 170 quad? . . . The best engineering brains in the country throw up their hands at the thought of having to produce 170 quad in another two dozen years.[14]

. . . . What we are faced with today represents the most massive change in the way humanity lives on this planet that has ever taken place. Morever, it will be in the shortest time.[15]

. . . . This energy squeeze is ab-

solutely real. It will continue to tighten like a vise even with the best cooperation of the Middle East oil producers."[16]

An unregulated free market in energy production and distribution would have prevented the problem in the first place. The Federal Reserve Bank of St. Louis', July 1977 **Review**, took an exhaustive look at the energy crisis. In an article entitled, "The Nature and Origins of the U.S. Energy Crisis", Jai-Hoon Yang concluded,

> *"The history of U.S. energy markets reveals that the roots of the current crisis have been nutured by past public policy measures. These policies were adopted in response to demands by segments of the energy industry for protection from the rigors of market competition. The crisis is rooted in the supplanting of the market mode of competition by the political mode.*[17]
>
> . . . . *It is ironic that those who now call for deregulation of the energy market are the ones that had successfully sought most of the existing regulations.*
>
> *. . . And we seem to forget that an unfettered energy market could, and still can, bring forth ever expanding supplies of energy from higher-cost conventional sources and more exotic, alternate sources.*"[18]

Deregulation of the energy industry can solve the problem long-term. Short-term, there could be serious problems.

Myers brought to light the words of Dr. Arthur M. Bueche, Vice-President of Research and Development at General Electric. Dr. Bueche, in a March 1977 address entitled, "The Hard Truth About Energy," stated, "'We can easily be slipping into an unimaginable catastrophe. To be blunt, I am not ruling out the very real possibility of social upheaval and revolution.'"[19]

The emotion and outcries, as we travel along our collision course with these crises, has all the earmarks of a market approaching a peak, just like the sugar market in 1974. One of two things can happen. Supply will increase - new water sources, more and better food production and distribution, new energy sources. Or, there can be a decrease in demand, which could be realized by a recession/depression and/or a reduction in the number of people on earth. The specter of T.R. Malthus - warfare, famine, pestilence, and disease comes into view.

Supply will solve part of the problem. That the problem is unlikely to be cured in time to avoid severe disruption is soberly stated in famed economist Robert Heilbroner's, **An Inquiry Into the Human Prospect.** The predicament and irrationality of men while in crisis was clearly revealed in Professor Pitirim Sorokin's 1942 classic, **Man and Society in Calamity.** Simply put, time has pretty much run out on solving the problems, and since the nature of the beast has been known since at least the early 1960's, it is probable the problems will be solved only when they engulf us. This heavily weights the odds in favor of a Malthusian solution.

Archeological Professor at the University of Michigan, George E. Mendenhall, has discovered that following the 10th generation in every civilization, chaos hits. He states, " 'Almost always a combination of the Four Horsemen of the Apocalypse' - famine, death, war, pestilence has caused the destruction. It's our turn now.' "[20]

Edward T. Hall, professor of anthropology at Northwestern University and author of **The Hidden Dimension,** studied overcrowding and concluded that it makes people behave like rats. When rats become overcrowded, dominant males become violent, attacking others and inflicting wounds on themselves. Other rats lose their social orientation and disease sets in. Hall declares that sustained crowding causes " 'physical weakening, sometimes rage and violence or extreme passivity, a rise in sexual abberations, and a breakdown of orderly group behavior.' "[21] Beverly T. Mead, psychiatrist at Creighton University, notes, " 'Crowding literally makes people sick.' "[22]

It is the conviction here that the resource crisis in the basics of survival - water, food, energy - will be solved before as well as during the real shortages, and that the crisis won't come anywhere near the proportions presently imagined. Rather, like a market topping out, it will be remedied partially by a reduction in demand, fewer people. One of the agents of this reduction is warfare. The primary trend of mankind is to go to war to resolve conflicts. There is no indication of a change in the primary trend.

Chapter VI

Civilization Cycles and War

Historian Arnold Toynbee viewed civilizations from a cyclical perspective. "Societies" rose, existed as civilizations, and then crumbled. The system was one of growth, breakdown, and then dissolution. Toynbee believed that man achieved civilization by responding correctly to difficult challenges. Thus, he formulated the idea of "challenge and response". A growing civilization has a challenge. Its response to the challenge is successful. The response then generates another and different challenge which must be met with a successful response. When the civilization fails to meet a new challenge, growth ceases and breakdown follows. "The challenge continues through successive but temporary attempts to meet it in a 'rout-rally-rout-rally-rout' pattern. Three and one-half beats of the rout-rally-rout rhythm seem to be typical of a number of disintegrating societies.' "[1]

Toynbee's studies revealed that civilizations grow as the result of the activity and thought of the creative minorities, and that **internal,** not external factors were the basis of growth. In other words, it was the conclusion of the greatest historian of the 20th Century that growth is determined by individual initiative and creativity, not by focusing upon the will of the majority as exercised by government. Toynbee saw growth being realized by overcoming material obstacles, which allowed greater energy of response. The masses imitate the experiences of creative minorities.[2]

Toynbee also discovered that internal rather than external factors are responsible for the civilization's decline. The nature of the breakdown can be summed up in three points: The creative minority fails to be creative, and then becomes a dominant minority; the majority, in turn, withdraws its allegiance and imitation ceases; the society as a whole loses its social unity.[3]

Toynbee regarded breakdown as "the nemesis of creativity".

"He applies this in three areas; the idolization of an ephemeral self, institution, and technique. The leaders of successful response tend to rest on their past achievements and therefore are ill-prepared to meet the next challenge. The intoxication of successful violence [NFL football], militarism, or triumph is the suicide of civilization."[4]

Toynbee saw the disintegration of civilizations to be at hand when,

"The 'creative minority' now changes to a 'ruling minority' and the masses into a 'proletariat' (a group which has no share in the civilization of its society). The 'schism' has occurred and broken the social body into three parts: dominant minority, internal proletariat, and external proletariat. The dominant minority develops a universal state for it is in this group that the legists and administrators are found. The internal proletariat, composed of 'stateless exiles', exercises its remaining creativity in the development of a universal church. The external proletariat develops into barbarian war bands and fights against the empire of the ruling minority.[5]

The 'time of trouble' is now in full swing for that society. There may be periods of 'rally' but the 'rout' is destined to prevail. The 'Indian summer' peace of the universal state is of short duration. Great men

may indeed appear on the scene, and Toynbee distinguishes five kinds of 'saviours of society'. The 'creative genius' once leading successful responses to challenges during a period of growth, now appears as a saviour from the disintegrating society. The 'saviour with the sword' arises from the dominant minority but proves ephemeral in the end. There may also arise the 'saviour with the time machine' who appeals to the past or future but ends up taking the sword and shares a similar fate. The 'philosopher masked by a king' will offer Platonic solutions but is doomed by his detachment from all but the ruling minority. Finally, the 'God incarnate in a man' may appear to have found a new religion but history has shown his imperfect solutions to be futile . . . ."[6]

Historian Oswald Spengler in his **Decline of the West** viewed the history of civilizations cyclically. The early rise of a Culture was the Springtime. The maturity of the Culture Spengler called the Summer and Autumn. The final period of the Culture was described as the Winter, or the Civilization, when the Culture was frozen. Spengler found that similar events seemed to happen at about the same points in each Culture. Architecture, mathematics, painting, music, the physical sciences, politics - all seemed to appear at identical points. City building occurred at about the same time. ". . . Feudal rule of the elite passed into democracy, then into mobocracy, then into Caesarism at the same points on all the cultural graphs that Spengler compiled."[7] Spengler saw a period of about 1,000 years between the Spring of a Culture and its ultimate Civilization.

"The wintertime of a Culture - its old age - is for Spengler the stage which he calls Civilization. It is the time of great city developments. It is here that he sees Caesarism inevitably developing.

Writing his great thesis during the course of the

first World War, Spengler felt quite certain that war would be only the first of many to come. For his charts showed our life in the awful age of 'Contending States', when the dictators would arise. He was equally certain that Democracy would shortly give way under the Caesar's march; the Caesars destroyed both Democracy and Money.[8]

. . . . Spengler, were he alive in 1940, would now perhaps recognize in Hitler the first of his Faustian Caesars, under whom he foresaw the world trembling, the money collapsing, and the blood streaming . . . ."[9]

A little known French historian, Amaury De Riencourt, made a fascinating philosophical and historical study entitled, **The Coming Caesars.** Along the same lines as Toynbee and Spengler, Riencourt saw Civilizations in terms of cycles. And he also saw the rise of large cities as the mark of the maturity of the Civilization, a prelude to war, internal strife, and eventually Caesar.

As maturity follows youth so Civilization follows Culture.

"Culture predominates in young societies awakening to life, grows like a young organism endowed with exuberant vitality, and represents a new world outlook. It implies original creation of new values, of new religious symbols and artistic styles, of new intellectual and spiritual structures, new sciences, new legislations, new moral codes. It emphasizes the individual rather than society, original creation rather than preservation and duplication, prototypes rather than mass production, an aesthetic outlook on life rather than an ethical one. Culture is essentially trail-blazing.

Civilization, on the other hand, represents the crystallization on a gigantic scale of the preceding Culture's deepest and greatest thoughts and styles,

HOW CULTURES GROW—"CONTEMPORARY" POLITICAL EPOCHS IN FOUR CULTURES

	Pre-Cultural Period: PRIMITIVE FOLK. . . . TRIBES AND THEIR CHIEFS. . . . AS YET NO "POLITICS" AND NO "STATE"	
NAME OF CULTURE		I · EARLY PERIOD *Organic articulation of political existence. The two prime classes (noble and priest). Feudal economics — purely agrarian values*
EGYPTIAN	Thinite Period [Menes] (3400–3000)	OLD KINGDOM (2900–2400) Feudal conditions of IVth Dynasty. Increasing power of feudatories and priesthoods. The Pharaoh as incarnation of Ra. — VIth Dynasty. Break-up of the Kingdom into heritable principalities. VIIth and VIIIth Dynasties, interregnum.
CLASSICAL	Mycenean Age [Agamemnon] (1600–1100)	DORIC PERIOD (1100–650) The Homeric kingship. Rise of the nobility. [Ithaca, Etruria, Sparta]. — Aristocratic synoecism. Dissolution of kinship into annual offices. Oligarchy.
CHINESE	Shang Period (1700–1300)	EARLY CHOU PERIOD (1300–800) The central ruler [Wang] pressed hard by the feudal nobility. — (934–904). I-Wang and the vassals. (842). Interregnum.
WESTERN	Frankish Period [Charlemagne] (500–900)	GOTHIC PERIOD (900–1500) Roman-German Imperial period. Crusading nobility. Empire and Papacy. — Territorial princes. Renaissance towns. Lancaster and York. (1254). Interregnum.
APPROXIMATE TIME INTERVALS	— *About 500 Years* —	— *About 500 Years* —
		1. Feudalism. Spirit of countryside and countryman. The "City" only a market or stronghold. Chivalric-religious ideals. Struggles of vassals amongst themselves and against overlords. 2. Crisis and ... of patriarchal forms. Fr... ...lism to aristocratic State...

SPRING

Not drawn to scale

44

Culture:

NAME OF CULTURE	II · LATE PERIOD *Actualizing of the matured State-idea. Town versus countryside. Rise of Third Estate ("Bourgeoisie"). Victory of money over landed property*		
EGYPTIAN	XIth Dynasty. Overthrow of the baronage by the rulers of Thebes. Centralized bureaucracy-state.	MIDDLE KINGDOM (2150–1800) XIIth Dynasty (2000–1788). Strictest centralization of power. Court and finance nobility.	(1788–1680). R... ...nd military g... ... Decay of the ... ...ll potentates, in some ... sprung from the people.
CLASSICAL	Sixth Century. First Tyrannis. [Cleisthenes, Periander, Polycrates, the Tarquins]. The City-State.	IONIC PERIOD (65... The pure Polis ...tism of the Demos). A ...olitics. Rise of the ti... ...e. Themistocles, Peric...	Fourth Century. Social revolution and Second Tyrannis [Dionysius I, Jason of Pherae, Appius Claudius the Censor]. *Alexander.*
CHINESE	Period of the "Protec... Ming-Chu (685–591) ...he Congresses of Prince... ...).	...TE CHOU PERIOD (800–500) Chun-Chiu period ("Spring" and "Autumn," 590–480). Seven powers. Perfection of social forms [Li].	(480). Beginning of the Chan-Kwo period. (441). Fall of the Chou dynasty. Revolutions and annihilation-wars.
WESTERN	Dyna... ...mily-power, and the Fr... [Richelieu, Wallenstein, ...well] about 1630.	BAROQUE PERIOD (1500–1800) Ancien Régime. Rococo. Court nobility of Versailles. Cabinet politics. Habsburg and Bourbon. Louis XIV. Frederick the Great.	End of Eighteenth Century. Revolution in America and France [Washington; Fox, Mirabeau, Robespierre]. *Napoleon.*
APPROXIMATE TIME INTERVALS	- - *About 300 Years* - -		
	3. Fashioning of a world of States of strict form. Frondes.	4. Climax of the State-form ["Absolutism"]. Unity of town and country ["State" and "Society"—the "three estates"].	5. Break-up of the State-form. Revolution and Napoleonism. Victory of the city over the countryside, of the "people" over the privileged, of the intelligentsia over tradition, of money over policy.

AUTUMN

SUMMER

Civilization:

THE BODY OF THE PEOPLE, NOW ESSENTIALLY URBAN IN CONSTITUTION, DISSOLVES INTO FORMLESS MASS. . . . MEGALOPOLIS AND PROVINCES. . . . THE FOURTH ESTATE ("MASSES") — INORGANIC AND COSMOPOLITAN

NAME OF CULTURE	↓ OUR PRESENT POSITION		
	WINTER		
EGYPTIAN	[1788]–1580). Hyksos period. Deepest decline. Dictatures of alien generals [Chian]. After 1600, definitive victory of the rulers of Thebes.	(1580–1350). XVIIIth Dynasty. Thuthmosis III.	(1350–1205). XIXth Dynasty. Sethos I. Rameses II.
CLASSICAL	(300–100). Political Hellenism. From Alexander to Hannibal and Scipio royal all-power; from Cleomenes III and C. Flaminius (220) to C. Marius — radical demagogues.	(100–0–100). Sulla to Domitian. Cæsar, Tiberius.	(100–300). Trajan to Aurelian. Trajan, Septimius Severus.
CHINESE	(480–230). Period of the "Contending States." (288). The Imperial title. The imperialist statesmen of Tsin. (From 289). Incorporation of the last states in the Empire.	(250–0–26). House of Wang-Cheng and Western Han Dynasty. (221). Augustus-title [Shi] of Emperor Hwang-Ti. (140–80). Wu-ti.	(25–220 A.D.). Eastern Han Dynasty. (58–71). Ming-ti.
WESTERN	(1800–2000). Napoleon to the World-War. "System of Great Powers," standing armies, constitutions. Twentieth-century transition from constitutional to informal sway of individuals. Annihilation-wars. Imperialism.	(2000–2200).	(After 2200).
APPROXIMATE TIME INTERVALS	— 200 Years —	— 200 Years —	— ??? —
	1. Domination of Money—"Democracy." Economic powers permeating the political forms and authorities.	2. Formation of Cæsarism. Victory of force-politics over money. Increasing primitiveness of political forms. Inward decline of the nations into a formless population, and constitution thereof as an Imperium of gradually-increasing crudity of despotism.	3. Maturing of the final form. Private and family policies of individual leaders. The world as spoil. Enfeeblement of the imperial machinery, against young peoples eager for spoil, or alien conquerors. Primitive human conditions slowly thrust up into the highly-civilized mode of living.

From E.F. Dakin's, _Today and Destiny_ (Oswald Spengler's, _The Decline of the West)_ Source - The Foundation for the Study of Cycles - 1948[10]

living on the petrified stock forms created by the parent Culture, basically uncreative, culturally sterile, but efficient in its mass organization, practical and ethical, spreading over large surfaces of the globe, finally ending in a universal state under the sway of a Caesarian ruler: . . .

Civilization aims at the gradual standardization of increasingly large masses of men within a rigidly mechanical framework - masses of 'common men' who think alike, feel alike, thrive on conformism, are willing to bow to vast bureaucratic structures, and in whom the social instinct predominates over that of the creative individual . . . .[11]

. . . . *Rome experienced a succession of New Deals,* . . .

New Deals take place when dynamic expansion is over, when the frontier comes to an end, when expansive sources of new wealth are exhausted, when the problem becomes one of distribution and organization rather than bold creation . . .[12]

. . . . *In all cases, these Civilization-people had a more democratic social structure than their cousins in the Old Culture areas. They were all strong, practical, self-disciplined men who were far less individualized than their Culture-cousins, individually uncreative but collectively powerful, men who borrowed from the parent Culture all the ethical, legalistic notions on which to build enduring Civilizations* . . .

These Civilization-people all emphasized the Rule of Law with a rigor unknown in former Culture days, and took a legalistic view on all human relations . . . .[13]

. . . . *Like a giant wheel of destiny, this cyclical rhythm* . . . *has operated in the past with unfailing regularity* . . . .[14]

. . . . It will avail us nothing to deny that such a cyclical rhythm exists - indeed, it is the best way of making sure that we will be its victims."[15]

Riencourt noted that the times of transition from Culture to Civilization and the rule of Caesar was marked by war. He states,

"While Culture slowly draws closer to the end of its historical development and while its philosophic outlook collapses into conflicting and discordant doctrines, political and social upheavals of great magnitude begin to sweep its world. All Cultures have thus ended in a chaos of 'world wars' and revolutions . . ."[16]

. . . . The great epochs of history are dramatic watersheds, the final world-conflagrations that put an end to great Cultures torn apart by their inner contradictions and call forth the establishment of Civilizations. Growing revulsion against the cataclysmic disorders which corrode their respective societies, growing distrust of all philosophies and ideologies, a gradual return to religion and revival of religious faith, and a flight from the dangerous liberty into the strong hands of capable Caesars - these are the hallmarks of this era of transition. And nothing is as significant as the voluntary surrender of that measure of freedom without which no true Culture would ever have developed. Democratic equality has done away with hereditary aristocracies everywhere, and in all cases, gigantic bureaucracies recruited 'democratically' take their place - the most convenient tools in the hands of the Caesars . . . . The growth of Caesarism is always closely related to the destruction of the aristocracies . . . ."[17]

Toynbee confirms with his comments on the "Time of Trouble".

" 'If the analogy between our Western

Civilization's modern history and other Civilization's 'Times of Troubles' does extend to points of chronology, then a Western 'Times of Troubles' which appears to have begun sometime in the sixteenth century may be expected to find its end sometime in the twentieth century; and this prospect may well make us tremble' ".[18]

What can be said about the United States today considering the perspective of Toynbee, Spengler, and Riencourt?

Toynbee has already stated that, " '. . . a Western 'Times of Troubles' which appears to have begun sometime in the sixteenth century may be expected to find its end in the twentieth century; and this prospect may well make us tremble.' "[19] Has government's pervasive expansion killed the drive of the creative minority? Is the creative minority now the dominant minority in the form of multinationals and banks? Has the majority become basically apathetic, uninvolved with governmental processes? Do individuals within the United States focus their primary activity on self-gratification? Has bureaucracy become the norm? The answers are sobering.

What about Spengler's view? When will the torch pass from democracy, to mobocracy, to Caesarism? Is the United States in the Wintertime of its Culture? Is the United States a Civilization? This is a time of great city development. The money of the United States is in the process of being destroyed.

And how about Riencourt? Does the United States exhibit the characteristics of a Civilization? Does the United States emphasize society, preservation and duplication, mass production? Is its industry spread over large sections of the globe (multinationals)? Are there masses of "common men" who bow to bureaucratic structures? Has the United States experienced New Deals? Is democratic equality the accepted standard? If so, then the time of war and Caesar is upon the United States.

Chapter VII

The Cities and Civil War

In previewing the potential for civil unrest in the United States, one necessarily focuses on the cities - the nerve center of the American civilization. Some 80% of the population of the United States lives within the 100 largest cities. Thus, the effects of climatic changes, monetary problems, economic recessions, etc., and the resultant changing expectations, are more fully realized in metropolitan areas, and manifested through mass action.

The cities thrive on a complex of sophisticated, sensitive, fragile, and interdependent life support systems. Given even a minor breakdown in the system, the powderkeg is now subject to explosion as was witnessed by the 1977 New York City blackout. The cities' populations are the most exposed to a breakdown in the distribution system, for they depend entirely upon the system for survival. They are the farthest removed from providing for their own subsistence.

Roberto Vacca, in his alarming book, **The Coming Dark Age,** foresaw the problem,

> ". . . *our great technological systems of human organization and association are continuously outgrowing ordered control: they are now reaching critical dimensions of instability . . . a chance concomitance of stoppages in the same area*

*could start a catastrophic process that would
paralyze the most developed societies and lead to the
deaths of millions of people . . . .*[1] . . . .
*It seems very likely . . . that the most developed
nations are on the way toward breakdown on a large
scale . . . ."*[2]

Roberto Vacca is fully qualified to make such remarks.
He is a mathematician, an authority in the field of electronic systems and computers, president of an electronic
systems firm in Rome, and a former visiting professor at
Cambridge and Harvard.

It is indeed ironic that the independence of the city
dwellers, which has contributed to an alienation and isola-
tion of individuals, is based upon a slave-like dependence
on a life support system which is also susceptible to
sabotage. The utilities (water, gas, electrical, etc.), as well
as the distribution system, could be rendered unusable in
each city by less than 10 well trained guerrilla fighters. In
such a case, the neighborhoods could turn into a frightening jungle of individual and family self-defense efforts,
since mutual trust, promulgated by interdependence, is
non-existent. The problem is compounded by a rootless
mobile society and the concomitant destruction of the extended family and family unit, the basis of society.

A quick word on the family is in order. Paul Popenoe,
founder of the American Institute of Family Relations,
stated, " 'No society has every survived after its family life
deteriorated.' "[3] Carle Zimmerman of Harvard commented, " 'The extinction of faith in the familistic system
is identical with the movements . . . in Rome about A.D.
150 . . . the change in the faith and belief in family systems
was associated . . . with enormous crises in the very
civilizations themselves.' "[4] Gibson Winter, sociologist at
the U. of Chicago, wrote in **Love and Conflict,**

" 'A society depends upon stable people . . . . People are stable when they grow in an atmosphere of love and order. . . . These are the gifts bestowed upon us by our families. A disordered family cannot produce the stable and responsible people who are essential to the daily business of a great country.

A healthy family is not an option for a society. It is a life-and-death matter. We can overlook this crisis for a generation or two. The undermining of the character of a people takes time. Then it begins to accumulate and symptoms of disorder appear on every side. The amount of mental disturbance throughout the society begins to rise rapidly. The reign of lawlessness penetrates to every corner of the society. Vandalism becomes commonplace. Respect for authority in school and family disappears . . .

These are signs of instability . . . . They cannot be remedied so long as the family is uprooted and disordered.' "[5]

In 1977, after a five-year study on the way children grow up in America, a Carnegie Corporation research team concluded that parents have been "dethroned" and no longer control their children's development.[6] The United States is vulnerable.

There are some other side problems, as well. Margaret Mead, anthropologist, stated in an interview with **The Christian Science Monitor,**

" 'When there is a degree of breakdown in established institutions, there is a proliferation of superstition, an outbreak of astrology, soothsaying, divination, . . . It happened in the Middle Ages and at

the end of Rome. Whenever there is an end of an
epoch, there is a proliferation of this sort of thing.' "[7]

J.D. Unwin of Oxford and Cambridge wrote in his anthropological study, **Sex and Culture,** " 'Any human society is free to choose either to display great energy or to enjoy sexual freedom; the evidence is that it cannot do both for more than one generation.' "[8] How far has the society come? Compare today with 1956 when families fought over whether Elvis Presley could be watched on the Ed Sullivan Show because of his suggestive movements.

The middle class is under assault. A normal probability distribution falls under a bell-shaped curve. The area between the first standard deviations, 68.3%, is the middle class in a free society - highly mobile, widely dispersed, with job and salary variations fulfilling the requirements of random numbers in the distribution. This middle class, the largest area under the bell-shaped curve, traditionally provides the stability in society. Traditionally, there are a few rich, a few poor, and a large middle class. The middle class is the productive segment of the society. It is being devastated by inflation, and is literally and figuratively caught in the middle. The poor receive welfare and other aid. The rich have the best shot at investment opportunity, tax advantages, and legal counsel. If the middle class is destroyed, and that is the trend presently, then at some point in time they will rebel. This can be expected when it is realized that there is little to be gained by individual in- itiative, or when their way of life is threatened.

The cities bear the brunt of the problems of the family and the middle class, for in the cities, due to sheer numbers and concentration of people, the problems are amplified.

Howard J. Ruff, in the September 1976 issue of **The Ruff Times,** summarized other reasons why the cities are in trouble and ripe for civil unrest. Ruff declared,

"1. We have raised expectations in the minds of

our citizens . . . It is assumed that if something is desirable, it is automatically possible. We have chosen to offer benefits to people, such as welfare and unemployment insurance, which has drawn them to the cities like flies. It has drawn the poor, the uneducated, the economically dislocated, the lazy, and the criminal. It has created a set of circumstances which perpetuates their problems . . . .

. . . Because we were not able to tolerate short-term suffering, we have given ourselves insoluble long-term problems.

2. . . . when the government solves a problem, it creates two problems of equal or greater dimension . . . government is the enemy of our cities, and the more money it ladles out, the greater the harm done.

3. City neighborhoods have moved toward one-race groupings, forming inbred, hostile ghettos with a garrison mentality toward the rest of the world . . . . It holds the seeds of race war.

4. The quality of life in the cities is diminishing as much of its citizens' resources are devoted to the simple maintenance of food and shelter, and little is available for the development of the cultured activities which have always been judged as man's greatest accomplishments.

5. We are seeing a great exodus of corporations, jobs, and middle-class population from the cities, leaving a sharply eroding tax-base and increasing deficit.

6. We have accumulated a staggering amount of municipal debt - over $200 billion. History records no instance of a debt of this proportion having been paid off. It has always been repudiated . . . .

7. It has endangered the safety of the nation's banking system, . . .

8. The G.I. Bill of Rights may be one of the major causes of the troubles . . .

9. Crime in the cities is out of control, and some cities have become jungles . . . .

10. The schools have ceased to teach and our cities are turning out functional and economic illiterates who do not understand how the system works and they are the voters who elect those who will have their hand on the spending throttle — the very people who are destroying the cities through their misguided legislation and policies.

11. And last of all, narcotics are sapping the strength of our cities by increasing the crime rate many times."[9]

Ruff went on to discuss how government has destroyed the South Bronx, an area with a population of over 500,000. He noted that the South Bronx has experienced 68,456 fires in the last 5½ years (33 fires a night), the population has dropped 20% in the last five years; there crime pays, welfare destroys work incentive and breaks up families, and minimum wage laws kill job opportunities. Welfare recipients are 28% of the population, 60% are unemployed, and the place looks like Berlin after World War II.

Ruff stated that the start of the trouble was in 1943, when the Emergency Price Control Act was passed, which froze rents. People began to take rent controls as a right. It wrecked rental housing. Landlords lost money due to the frozen rents, and thus maintenance declined as taxes and cost of maintenance increased. Tenants moved out. The neighborhood became a "low rent district". Blacks from the South and Puerto Ricans flooded the area. If there were no jobs, there was always welfare. The business climate became unattractive. Government levied taxes which soaked the business community. Businesses moved. Jobs were lost. Unemployment swelled. Burglaries increased 700%, assaults 420% in ten years. Federal government money came in - $3 million for an experimental Social Services Center, $16 million for a Family Health Care Center, $77 million for a Model Cities program, $250 million for a hospital. A $413 million, 15,000-unit apartment complex was sponsored by United Housing Foundation, State financed with subsidized rents. Initially it attracted 50,000 residents. It was a horrible failure. In early 1975 alone 5400 apartment units were abandoned. Insurance fires became frequent. Buildings were stripped after they were burned. Drug addicts then occupied the premises. Police could not handle all the crime. The odds of a felony conviction were less than 1%.[10]

Ruff quoted a **Business Week** editorial,

" 'The problems of New York City are not unique. By 1980, every one of the 30 cities in the U.S. with a population of more than one million will be in financial distress to some degree. These big cities are in big declines. They are all adding services and increasing public payrolls, while the economic base deteriorates.' "[11]

Ruff states, "I believe we will see a class war, and racial stresses may trigger it.[12]

.... I believe that we will find ourselves in this position sometime between 1980 and 1985."[13]

Is there any wonder New York City erupted during Blackout 1977? There is little question presently that the situation can only go from bad to worse. Perhaps the subconscious of America senses the trouble ahead for our cities. Calvin Beale, a demographer at the U.S. Dept. of Agriculture, has noted that aware Americans are flocking from the cities to the country as never before. "It marks a turning point in our society."[14] For the first time since 1920, rural areas are increasing in population while the metropolitan areas are holding steady or decreasing.

Chapter VIII

Minorities, Business Cycles, and Cycles of War

Of special concern during the upcoming period are the actions of the minority groups. These "special interest" groups make up 13.4% of the United States population, most of whom reside in the cities.[1] For the first time since the Kennedy/Johnson era, minorities again have had their expectations elevated. This time the prophet of hope was Mr. Jimmy Carter. He exchanged promises for votes. Last cycle, reneging on promises resulted in the violence of the 1960's. This time, considering the old age and weakened condition of the master business cycle, the tables are set for quite a spill. The 50-year crest of the American economy is like the peak in the stock market when, at last, the stocks that have refused to rally all along, do so. At the economic crest, finally the expectations of the minorities are uplifted. Then is the time, when all seems well, that the bottom falls out. Smashed expectations can be an exploding grenade of violence.

Notice Hutner's Cycles of Optimism and Pessimism (page 61). Its composition of the three important cycles turns down in 1980. The previous peaks, 1970 and 1973, coincided perfectly with the summit of the then four-year economic cycles that preceded recessions. The 1980 crest is a predictive bingo! It lines up with the time for violence forecast by McClelland in his earlier reviewed literature studies. It parallels the timing of monetary disruption and political unrest expected by Jensen and Sauers, as well as a time of climatic instability according to Winkless and Browning. It is also when the Kondratieff Wave's "grace plateau" turns down. The visionaries and prophets additionally view this period as a time of trouble.

The evidence does not stop there! The present period is the peak period of a number of fifty year cycles. R.N. Elliott in his well known work, **Nature's Law**, noted a 55-year Fibonacci number cycle in commodity prices.[3] They inflated in 1864, 1919, and in 1973-74. Wheat, the staff of life, runs in a 54-year cycle that has been traced back to the 1500's.[4] It peaked in 1974. Cycle Sciences Corporation of San Francisco, in their October 1, 1976 newsletter, explained that the 9-year, 18-year, 54-year, and 100-year business cycles are all headed into the pit.[5] Bob McGregor, in a "Special Report" prepared for the August 15, 1977 issue of **World Money Analyst** graphically depicted the "grand super cycle" of the U.S. stock market from 1789 to 1975. He showed that the U.S. stock market has been in a "very, very long term bull market . . . ." In his opinion the market action from 1966 to the present, has, in real terms, formed a super bull top.[6] Last, but not least, is the 50-year cycle in Leviticus 25 of the **Bible's** Old Testament. Israel had seven, seven year cycles, plus one year - the year of Jubilee, the 50th year. This 50th year brought on a reversion of all possessions and parcels of land to the original family owners. The implications of the Jewish 50-year cycle is that about all the debt accumulation a society can stand prior to a major readjustment is 50 years. Also, it would seem that after 50 years, too much wealth has been accumulated by too few, and this must be reconciled. It has been 50 years since the Great Depression.

Norman Alcock, working with a composite cyclical index, confirmed the independent cycles. He stated that the composite cyclical index was, ". . . used to project the world economy for the next 25 years. A period of no-growth or stagnation is indicated."[7] Growth is the life's blood of the U.S. economy.

To the misfortune of the United States, the militant leaders of the NAACP, along with Vernon Jordan, executive director of the Urban League, have little knowledge or appreciation for this economic data. The minorities have been made promises. Mr. Carter has been accused of being anti-black. As Jordon stated before the July, 1977, Urban League National Convention,

" 'We have no full employment policy. We have no welfare reform policy. We have no national health policy. We have no urban revitalization policy. We have no aggressive affirmation action policy. We have no national solution to the grinding problems of poverty and discrimination.' "[8]

Rev. Jesse Jackson, national director of Operation Push, stated, " 'We will have to take to the streets again . . .' "[9] Lerone Bennett, Jr., senior editor of **Ebony Magazine** declared, " 'A whole generation is growing up in the slums . . . with no faith in American or African-American institutions.' "[10] **The Wall Street Journal,** in an article entitled, "To Black Leaders Moral Drift Is A Big Problem," noted, "Blacks in the slums, young and old, feel excluded by the system and oppressed by it."[11] Here Crane Brinton's **Anatomy of Revolution** comes to mind. The minorities have Great Expectations as a result of government promises. When the cold water of economic realism and political chicanery hits, it is doubtful that the reaction will be passive.

The very fact that minority groups have accepted so much welfare and other aid in the past has already triggered a psychological principle that results in violence. "There is a basic psychological law that an ego cannot be indebted with no means of repaying and not retaliate in some manner".[12] Another example of this is the foreign aid program pursued by the U.S. government which has dished out billions in foreign aid to undeveloped nations who have been unable to repay. As a result, the United States is now one of the "best hated" nations in history.

What influence has the communist movement had on the alienation of the minorities from the American system? In the latter half of the 1960's, Ms. Charlotte Phelps was an instructor in the Business School at the U. of Houston. Her speciality was economics and business values. It is no wonder she was charismatic, for she was trained in Cuba as a recruiter for black communist cell blocks in Houston, Texas. As a result of her activities, Ms. Phelps was sentenced to a 35-year term in the Texas penitentiary at Huntsville, Texas. It seems that Texans don't take too kindly to automatic weapons, grenades, and robberies on their streets!

Several U. of Houston students were indicted with her, students who had been recruited by her. Ms. Phelps' Business Values class was simply a communistic indoctrination program geared to the destruction of the cultural values of her younger students. Once the "cultural black box" was shattered, Ms. Phelps could rebuild the communist version. At that time, she stated that the next U.S. revolution was scheduled for the late 1970's.

61

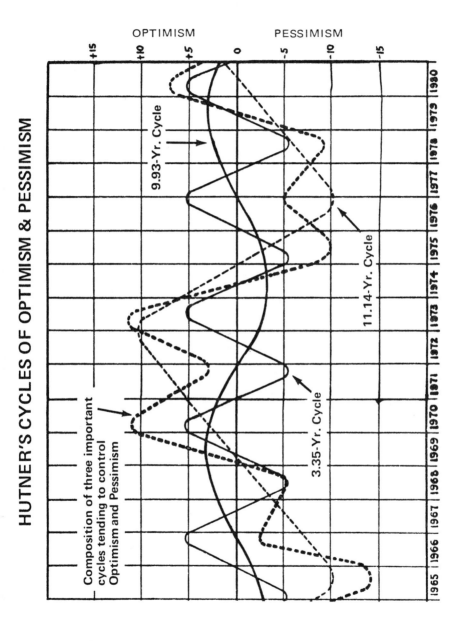

Source - Foundation for the Study of Cycles - 1975[2]

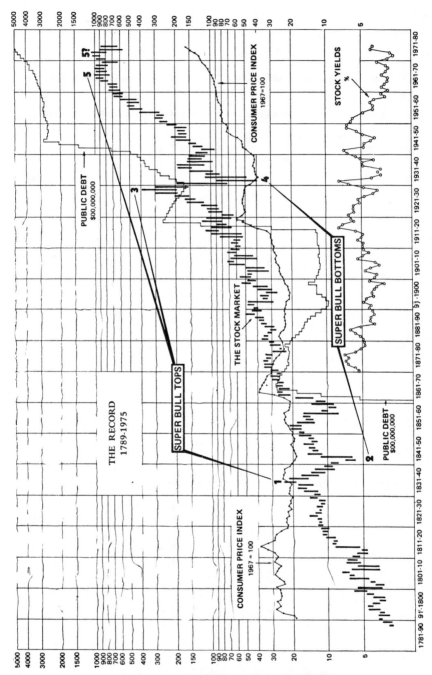

THE RECORD
1789-1975

SUPER BULL TOPS

SUPER BULL BOTTOMS

PUBLIC DEBT
$00,000,000

PUBLIC DEBT
$00,000,000

CONSUMER PRICE INDEX
1967=100

CONSUMER PRICE INDEX
1967 = 100

THE STOCK MARKET

STOCK YIELDS
%

Source - World Money Analyst - 1977[13]

Chapter IX

The Kondratieff Wave/Cycle and War

Nikolai D. Kondratieff, a Russian economist and Director of the Conjuncture Institute of Moscow, in 1925 published his work on Western economic cycles. It has become popularly known as the Kondratieff Wave. Kondratieff's thesis is basically that the free world economy fluctuates in an economic cycle that peaks approximately every 54 years. He based his studies upon such items as industrial production, wages, wholesale prices, and interest rates. France, Great Britain, the United States, and Germany were the nations Kondratieff studied. Kondratieff actually stated that the cycle could vary between 48 and 60 years. That is logical. Cycles can extend, contract, and even sometimes disappear where human action is involved. It has been in more recent times that the Wave has been pinpointed to 54 years from peak to peak.

Kondratieff's work was not appreciated in Russia. His Wave implied that the capitalistic system was basically self-correcting, an idea contrary to Marx. Nikolai was exiled to a labor camp in Siberia as a result of his efforts.

The Western world, indoctrinated in the god of rationalism/reason (humanism), also did not take too kindly to Kondratieff's work. The very concept of a cycle falls in the school of economic determinism, which says, in effect, that man has little or no control over his destiny. The event will occur to fit the cycle. Cycle says, "Thumbs up," - thumbs up. Cycle says, "Thumbs down," - thumbs down, as it were. Obviously, this humbling revelation by Kondratieff did not set well with intellectuals and university professors. It made them look (particularly the fundamental economists) foolish at best, useless at worst.

In any case, the Wave runs roughly as follows: At the trough of the Wave there is a war. Then the Cycle moves up for slightly longer than 20 years. These are the good times, times of peace and prosperity. Next, there is a sharp drop off, such as occurred during 1974, followed by a plateau period of between 7-10 years. (There is also a war near the peak period.) After the plateau, it is all downhill for the next 20 years or so. See illustration next page.

Kondratieff is helpful in outlining the times from easy to difficult, the large swings from optimism to pessimism, from prosperity to depression, and from inflation to deflation. What is the concern here is the peak period. There is a peak approaching war (Indochina), a sharp drop off in the economy, followed by a prosperous plateau, and then a depression. Most Kondratieff theoreticians believe the Wave peaked in 1973, dropped off sharply in 1974, and the late 1970's is the plateau period. Possibly so.

The Indochina war does not prevent a subsequent war occurring. The present Kondratieff Wave is not in keeping with the previous U.S. wholesale prices' pattern of prior Kondratieff Waves. The divergence of U.S. wholesale prices (up) from the hypothetical Kondtarieff Wave peak opens to thought at least the possibility that another war could occur.

The world is interrelated now as never before through international trade. Yet, there is no international will to promote this interdependent free trade adequately. In fact, nations do not aggressively seek free trade. As the economy of a nation becomes weakened or threatened by imports, the nation/state takes whatever political

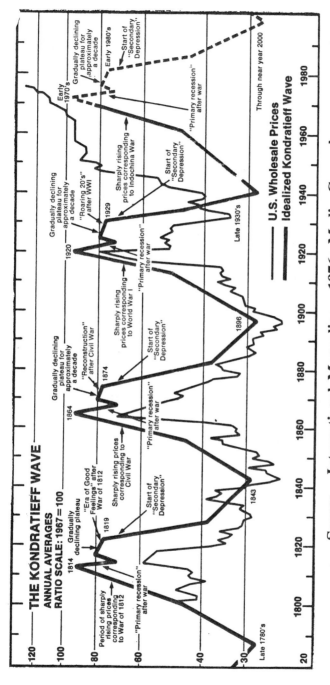

THE KONDRATIEFF WAVE

ANNUAL AVERAGES
RATIO SCALE: 1967 = 100

—— U.S. Wholesale Prices
━━ Idealized Kondratieff Wave

Source - International Moneyline - 1976; Media General
Financial Weekly - 1972[1]

measures are expedient to protect its own self-interest, or rather, its own perceived self-interest, by means of protective tariffs, embargoes, and trade wars - general protectionism (multinational pressure to the contrary). Presently, there is pressure in the United States for trade restrictions from the textile, apparel, and shoe industries. In Europe now, only 60% of the available capacity is being utilized in steel production. Japanese imported steel is blamed. The August 8, 1977 issue of **U.S. News and World Report** featured an article entitled, "Growing Worry Over World Trade War." This article noted, "A rush to erect trade barriers at national borders is the cause of mounting concern among business leaders in both the U.S. and Western Europe."[2] The international economy is becoming weaker. "Resurgent economic nationalism inside Europe - in fact, almost everywhere in the world - is considered a major factor in the crisis of confidence . . . . Says a high-placed source at Common Market headquarters, 'The dams are breaking.' "[3]

The August 11, 1977 **Wall Street Journal** feature article was entitled, "Global Commerce Expands More Slowly As Barriers to It Spread." From that article,

"World trade shows worrisome signs of a slow-down.

. . . Looking beyond 1977, there's concern that trade expansion could grind nearly to a halt.

. . . . Expanding international trade, of course, has been a main ingredient in the global prosperity marking the past couple of decades.

. . . . A major factor underlying the trade slowdown appears to be protectionism . . .

. . . . Protectionist measures to limit imports are proliferating.

. . . . This view is supported by a re-

cent report from the International Monetary Fund . . . the report finds that 'a greater proportion of world trade' recently has become subject to such restraints as import surcharges, quotas, trade-limiting pacts and various nontariff barriers."[4]

Earlier in 1977 Japanese Prime Minister, Takeo Fukuda, warned that protectionism could lead to another economic replay similar to the 1930's. Mr. Fukuda said, " '. . . The world economic situation following the 1973 oil crisis was quite similar to the developments of that particular time.' "[5] In the 1930's Fukuda observed, " '. . . major countries, one after another, abandoned the open economic system of free trade, switching to the closed system of protectionism.' "[6] In typical diplomatic fashion, Mr. Fukuda went on to state, " 'I am not suggesting that we are once again on the road to World War. Yet I feel deep anxiety about the social and political consequences with the world if we slide once again into protectionism, or a breakup of the world economy into trade blocks.' "[7]

As Ludwig von Mises put it in his economic treatise, **Human Action,** "The philosophy of protectionism is philosophy of war."[8] He also stated, "If men and commodities are prevented from crossing borderlines, why should not the armies try to pave the way for them?"[9]

There are some signs that the late 1970's are the plateau period of the Kondratieff Wave. The era has witnessed relatively good economic stability and good times, free of the severe inflation of the previous era. But the storm clouds of economic protectionism are building. And there are still rising prices, and economic expectations have not eased or retrenched on the part of the masses, which should have occurred during a plateau period. The caldron that bubbles below the apparently cool lid of today's cities can best be seen by the riots, burning, and looting during the New York City blackout of 1977. Beyond a shadow of a doubt, the violent activity of the minorities in New York City during the blackout laid to rest any hopes that, (a) the cities had solved their problems, or (b) during times of disruption, the population would remain calm. Civil unrest is still a major threat to domestic tranquillity as national economic protectionism is a threat to international peace. That the political climate is hardening against the minorities is apparent from the concern voiced by the ADA (Americans for Democratic Action). For 30 years, the ADA has been rating Congress on its voting record on civil rights issues. In 1977, the ADA issued its alarming report that in 80% of the crucial votes, Congress had voted against the civil rights issue as seen by the ADA.[10] Now 40% of the black teenagers in the United States are unemployed.

Shuman and Rosenau made an interesting observation about women's rights in their book, **The Kondratieff Wave.** They commented that the movement for female equality existed in the 1920's just prior to the depression of the 1930's, and did not reappear until the early 1960's. Ironically, the same thing had happened the century before when Susan B. Anthony gained popular support for women's rights in the 1850's prior to the Civil War.[11]

Enter Fibonacci. Leonardo Fibonacci was a brilliant Italian mathematician of the 13th century. He devised the phenomenal Fibonacci number series (1, 1, 2, 3, 5, 8, 13, 21, 34, 55, 89 . . .) which is found throughout the natural order and has been long admired by such great market analysts as R.N. Elliott (Elliott Wave). Examples of it are as follows: There are three primary colors. On the piano keyboard there are 8 white keys and 5 black keys, totaling 13. From the torso of the human body, there are 5 projections - head, 2 arms and 2 legs. Man has 5 fingers and toes, 5 senses. Birds have 5 projections from the torso. The ratio of 1.618 or .618 fascinated the Greeks. It is connected with the architecture of plants. It is called the

Golden Section. It played a critical part in the construction of The Great Pyramid Gizeh. The age of 21, a Fibonacci number, is the "wonderful" age of freedom.[12]

The library of Lambert-Gann Publishing Company has interesting information on Fibonacci that relates to this discussion. From that library,

"Fibonacci anticipated the coming of the time when the basic and intrinsic differences between male and female numbers may disappear. The two may become closer to one another: The male may become equivalent to the female: The male may acquire some of the characteristics typical of the female and vice versa; the female may acquire some of the characteristics which are typical of a male. Fibonacci thinking and writing approximately 7 centuries ago, viewed this development as indicating the entering on the part of the human race into one of its darkest periods of history, a period of confusion, chaos, violence, and death."[13]

The Equal Rights movement of the 1920's built upon Susan B. Anthony's base of the 1850's. The feminist movement of the 1970's has further built upon the base of the 1920's. (**R.N.** Elliott in his **Nature's Law** noticed that markets made three drives to a top. Considering the feminists' movement - 1850's, 1920's, 1970's - a top?) The gay liberation movement saw the light for its campaign from the success of the present feminist movement.

Only time will tell whether Fibonacci was correct in his observations concerning male and female. The leading European mathematician of his time saw the blending of such as a prelude to, "one of the darkest periods in history, a period of confusion, chaos, violence, and death."[14]

Chapter X

Cycles of War and the Military

As an offshoot of their research with climate, Winkless and Browning discovered, ". . . That the countries with the larger standing armies: (1) Start fewer wars, (2) Get dragged into fewer wars, (3) Win a greater percentage of the wars in which they become involved."[1] The present low level of the U.S. "standing army" is causing serious concern in military circles. The legendary Will Rogers once remarked that the best barometer of an approaching war was a reduction in the military forces by the United States. The August 9, 1977, **Wall Street Journal** headlined, "Achilles' Heel? Army Reserve Forces Are Falling Steadily: Pentagon is Worried." From that article,

". . . the National Guard and Reserve forces . . . who are supposed to reinforce active troops in wartime - are significantly below strength and shrinking every month.

. . . many Reserve and Guard units are far from ready to fight on short notice at a time when the Army increasingly is relying on such forces for combat support in case of war."[2]

The active duty personnel are not in much better shape. Illiteracy is becoming so bad in the Navy that it is difficult for that branch of the service to find the recruits necessary to carry out normal duties. In San Diego, for example, a recent study of Navy recruits revealed that 37% of the 23,-000 tested read below the 10th grade level.[3]

There are other less publicized problems, of a more serious nature. In 1974, a clean-cut and religious youth from Montana graduated from high school and "joined the Navy to see the world." He had a rude awakening. Home on leave, he wanted to go AWOL. He was afraid to go back to his ship. He had discovered a drug ring that was run by those in authority. After some soul searching, this young man returned to his ship under the conviction that if things didn't improve he would report the ring to higher authorities. He never had an opportunity to do so. He was found dead, hung by the neck one afternoon in the middle of the ship for all to see. The official report said suicide. The warning to all others aboard had been given.

Finally, in private conversations, the subject is raised about the potential problem, in time of crisis, of having a basically white officer corps, while the enlisted ranks are made up increasingly of minorities. More than one white officer lost his life in supposedly "friendly" company during Viet Nam.

What about the armament question? The Collins Report, entitled, "American and Soviet Military Strengths, Contemporary Trends Compared, 1970-76" was suppressed by staff members of the Senate Armed Services Committee because it revealed recent changes where the Soviet Union is now "clearly superior." Those areas are: air defense missiles, anti-ship missiles, armored fighting vehicles, artillery/rocket launchers, chemical/biological warfare, cold weather equipment, gas turbines for ships, ICBM payload and yields, mobile ballistic missiles, ship size vs. firepower, and tactical bridging. The report was prepared by John M. Collins of the Congressional Research Service at the Library of Congress. Collins has a reputation for excellence and factual work in defense related areas.[4]

The U.S. is the clear underdog in other areas as well.

"Some Soviet submarines now carry nuclear missiles with nearly twice the range of current U.S. models, enabling the Russians to hit many American targets without leaving home port, . . .

. . . . The United States is not expected to have a comparable seaborne missile until the Trident II becomes operational in the mid-1980's."[5]

"President Carter's decision to halt USAF/Boeing Minuteman 3 production and the NS-20 ICBM guidance system, on which final deliveries are scheduled for Nov. 1978, has caused alarm among American strategic planners, some of whom are convinced that the U.S. is moving towards reliance on a single strategic deterrent - submarine launched ballistic missiles."[6]

"NATO intelligence has learned of a new class Soviet ballistic missile submarine now being constructed at the Severodvinsk shipyard, 30 miles northwest of Archangel. Code-named Typhoon, the new sub is believed to be in the class of the U.S. Trident 2, which is scheduled for operations in the late 1980's by the U.S. Navy."[7]

A.P. Special Correspondent Peter Arnett and A.P. Military Writer Fred S. Hoffman, in a five-part series entitled, "Is American Ready to Fight a Conventional Land War?" stated,

"America's ability to fight a major conventional land, air and sea war has been seriously weakened by shortages in key weapons and ammunition and by other critical deficiencies.

The Pentagon has started corrective actions, but it will take from two to six years to cure most of the major shortcomings . . . . 'Stated frankly and simp-

ly, our Army is outgunned and inadequately equipped,' is the way one Army official put it.

'We have had to live with under equipped tactical fighter units, shortfall in airlift capability, an austere . . . air defense force . . . and persistent shortages of aircraft spare parts and some types of munitions,' said Gen. David Jones, Air Force Chief of Staff.

'It will take at least five or six years of concerted effort before the material condition of the entire fleet attains a sustainable satisfactory level', said the Defense Department, describing the Navy."[8]

Other highlights of the report include: (1) The Army needs 15,000 tanks in order to defeat Soviet armor. It only has 7,000. (2) The Army's War Reserve stocks of tanks, armored troop carriers, ammunition, anti-tank missiles, and self-propelled artillery are low. (3) The Air Force only has about half of the necessary advanced air-to-air missiles needed to duel Soviet fighter planes for control of the skies. (4) Few units of the Army National Guard and Reserve are rated ready for deployment. (5) The Reserve manpower is drying up. (6) Warplanes have been grounded due to lack of spare parts. (7) The operating effectiveness of warships have been severely cut by delayed overhauls. (8) Some of the new aircraft, ships, and other complex weapons have caused major problems due to poor reliability. (9) The U.S. military services are at the lowest manpower level since the Korean War. (10) The U.S. Navy, which is made up of 468 ships, is the smallest it has been since prior to the Japanese attack on Pearl Harbor in 1941.[9]

And what about the civil defense efforts? The U.S.S.R. is on a crash program to prepare for nuclear war. The U.S.S.R. has stockpiled grain, placed airport and missile installations underground, made massive underground civil defense preparations for the Russian population, and has even relocated industrial plants underground.[10]

On the other hand, the General Accounting Office has stated that the United States' poor civil defense planning makes it "questionable whether the government would continue to function" after a nuclear attack. The GAO stated that based upon the Defense Civil Preparedness Agency estimates, about 125 million Americans would be killed in a surprise nuclear attack.[11]

What have the "authorities" had to say about the chance of war? The prestigious Stockholm International Peace Research Institute released its 8th annual report in the summer of 1977 on the possibility of nuclear war. The report stated,

> *"The probability of a nuclear war is steadily increasing . . . is virtually inescapable . . . ."*[12]

> *Improved offensive and defensive strategic weapons and sizable nuclear arsenals could well lead to a situation in which adventurous political and military leaders in one or both of the great powers may perceive a chance of winning a strategic nuclear war."*[13]

The August 22, 1977, **U.S. News & World Report** stated, "U.S. - Soviet relations are **coolest in years.**" Secretary of State Vance has stated that relations between the U.S. and the U.S.S.R. are strained. Lt. General Graham, former director of the U.S. Defense Intelligence Agency, declared in an interview with **Defense & Foreign Affairs Digest** that we are "entering into a pre-war" period.[14]

Finally, the question must be asked, "What if they gave a war and nobody came?" At least, the question should be asked to the U.S.'s side of the conflict. The active duty forces are at minimal manpower requirements and are plagued by illiteracy, poor discipline, and drug problems, just for a start. The reserves are acknowledged as an "Achilles' Hell". The men who fought in Korea and Viet Nam aren't likely to be "suckered in" the third time around. Those who avoided the draft and were let "off the hook" have no reason to show up, should the draft be reinstituted. Certainly they would be let off the hook again. And what about volunteers and new draftees? Considering the no-win policy, the low credibility of the government, thanks to Mr. Nixon, among others, not to mention the deep suspicion of the military itself, it is a question that deserves some thought. What if the U.S. was involved in a war, a serious one, not a Viet Nam chess game? Could the nation pull together? The words of a folk song written **after** Viet Nam may well express the attitude of those who will be called on to fight in the coming "Time of Trouble". The lyrics should wrinkle a few brows.

The U.S. Military
(Everybody Smile for Me)

1. Commander, Commander,
   Commander-in-Chief.
   We know, oh we know, sir,
   Your stay here will be brief.
   Your concern for us must be remote,
   Historically soldiers seldom vote.
   Now, everybody smile,
   Everybody smile for me.

   Anchors, anchors, anchors away,
   Rusting away in the bottom of a bay . . .

   Chorus
   The U.S. Military,
   Everybody smile, say hara-kiri.
   A full month's leave and now good pay,
   C.O.D. for a M.I.A.
   Everybody smile for me,
   Everybody smile for me.

2. General, oh General,
   Won't you march this way.
   You've a chest full of ribbons,
   On display today.
   We won't ask how you got so far,
   You sold your soul for political stars.
   Now, everybody smile,
   Everybody smile for me.

   Off we go into the wild blue yonder,
   Delicate careers are to be pondered . . .

   Chorus
   The U.S. Military
   Everybody smile, say hara-kiri.
   Underarmed and overfed,
   Healthy, wealthy, dumb, and dead.
   Everybody smile for me,
   Everybody smile for me.

3. Soldier, oh soldier,
   You're the rank and file.
   Yes, you, of course, are
   The one who's been beguiled.
   You ask, "What should we fight for?
   We haven't won since the second World War."
   Now, everybody smile,
   Everybody smile for me.

   Over hill, over dale,
   Hear the echoes of our wails . . .

   Chorus
   The U.S. Military
   Everybody smile, say hara-kiri.
   A full month's leave and now good pay,
   C.O.D. for a M.I.A.
   Everybody smile for me,
   Everybody smile for me.

4. Politicos, Politicos,
   Way up on the Hill.
   Say, "Yes Sir, Yes Sir,
   Yes Sir, Three bags filled."
   Where are the men who could carry us far,
   Are we headed now for the third World War?

Now, everybody smile,
Everybody smile for me.

From the halls of Montezuma
You'll hear of the doom of . . .

Chorus
The U.S. Military
Everybody smile, say hari-hiri.
Underarmed and overfed,
Healthy, wealthy, dumb, and dead.
Everybody smile for me,
Everybody smile for me.

                                        Anonymous

Chapter XI

Prophets, Visionaries, and Cyles of War

The "sensitives" are members of the smallest minority in society. They either have the time, or make the time, to reflect on the past and present and its implications for the future. The philosophers, psychics, artists, composers, writers, poets and so on, are an aware elite. These individuals have an uncommonly well developed right half of the brain where the intuitive talent rests. They are generally more emotional, moody, naive, open, and trusting. The left hemisphere is far better developed in most people. Its skill is logical analysis. Its development is reinforced by the public school system. The electroencephalograph (EEG) identifies the wave patterns produced by the electrical impulses in the brain. Most adults have predominant activity in the Beta frequency. It is associated with the use of physical senses, and the ability to operate logically with physical ideas and concepts. On the other hand, the Alpha waves are associated with intuition and creative thinking. With the Alpha waves also comes the ability to control conscious thought, and the body.

The sensitives, taken as a group, have a different concept of time as well. To them, the concept of "ordinary time" does not exist. They operate in a fourth dimension. The psychics, for example, can see the "whole show" - the past, the present, and the future. They have the ability to transcend the "now".

Albert Einstein, in his theory of relativity, stressed that

time and space are relative concepts, not absolutes. He believed that the future and the past both exist at the same time. Therefore, motion must be defined relative to a specific frame of reference. It was Einstein's thought that the "now" present was only a more or less meaningless transition between the past and future. That the here and now is unreal is difficult to grasp at first. But time is an integrated whole. Only because man is alive, aware, and conscious, does he have a concept of time.

The concept of time should not be confused with the importance of timing. There is a "tide in the affairs of men." The Book of Ecclesiastes in the Old Testament of **The Bible** (KJV) states in chapter 3, verses 1-8,

> *"To every thing there is a season, and a time to every purpose under the heaven: A time to be born, and a time to die; a time to plant, and a time to pluck up that which is planted; A time to kill, and a time to heal; A time to break down, a time to build up; A time to weep, a time to laugh; A time to mourn, and a time to dance; A time to cast away stones, and a time to gather stones together; A time to embrace, and a time to refrain from embracing; A time to get, and a time to lose; a time to keep, and a time to cast away; A time to rend, a time to sew; a time to keep silence, and a time to speak; A time to love, and a time to hate; a time of war, and a time of peace."*

Timing in life is everything! Man is much more successful swimming with the tide than against it. There is a time for everything, but notice that within the concept of opposites, judgment is required. Whether to speak or keep silent requires wisdom and judgment. Man needs good judgment as well as the knowledge of the Time within which he is working in order to make the best decisions. For example, during the rise in gold prices during 1973, stock brokers who sold gold stocks to the public made a fortune. Their decision to sell was in harmony with Time and inflationary expectations. Those who persisted in selling gold stocks during 1976 found out what it meant to starve. Their decision was incorrect with respect to Time and investor preference.

Cycles focus on timing. And as mentioned previously, cycles are deterministic. The cycle is set. Some event will occur to confirm the cycle. Market analysts, known as technicians, focus upon price action in the market. They watch prices move, and then wait for the news to happen to justify the price movement. It is not always this way. Human free choice enters into the picture, and thus the price movements are probabilistic forecasters of the news. It seems that man's free will oscillates within the boundaries of predestination. And the concept of opposites plays a big part in judgments by man in directional time.

The action of the heavenly bodies is tied to human action, cycles, and timing. In Chapter 3, Jensen's study of the planets Saturn, Uranus, and Jupiter revealed their coordination with business cycles. The Russian scientist, Tchijevski, correlated human excitability with the 11-year sunspot cycle. This was discussed in Chapter 4. The late Burton H. Pugh, founder of the Market Forecaster Company revealed in 1929 "the great wheat secret". Buy wheat during the full moon phase. Its price will rise. Sell wheat during the new moon phase. Then wheat's price will drop. This technique made Pugh a fortune. He found it most successful during the months of September through May, if there was not some other overwhelming influence on the market.[1] Silver prices follow the same pattern as wheat. More babies are conceived on the full moon. More crime takes place. And then there is the **Farmer's Almanac.** When do farmers plant crops? What effect do tides have on earthquake and volcanic activity? The entire solar system is an integrated system. The action in one area affects other areas. It is important to see the whole interrelated system.

(This total, holistic approach in corporation analysis is called the systems approach. For example, if procurement is buying raw materials far in excess of requirements, it could be "suboptimizing", benefiting itself at the expense of the whole organization. In this example, production might instead need the funds for machine replacement.)

Man does not yet know all the effects, or even all the relationships that exist as a result of the gravitational and electromagnetic activity of planets. It is still an open field. The work of Lieutenant-Commander David Williams was discussed in Chapter 3. The Jupiter Effect was discussed in Chapter 4. These studies are considered by many to border on the occult. But man has traditionally looked upon the new and unknown with suspicion.

Congress laughed at Samuel Morse when he asked for $30,000 to build a telegraph line, even after he had demonstrated that it worked. The Wright brothers had many successful flights at Kitty Hawk before they received publicity. Eyewitness accounts of the flights were ignored. Louis Pasteur was criticized for his theories of germs causing diseases. Man does not like to change. He resists change. He will selectively filter the evidence rather than see it rationally if it means an unwanted or uncomfortable change.

The United States is particularly bad in this regard. It comes partially as a result of being a Civilization rather than a Culture. Cultures emphasize the individual, and encourage individual development and differences. One need only glance at the mass production public school system to see clearly that real development of personal idiosyncrasies is not the case in the United States. And how many really unusual names abound in the United

States? Television is the mass equalizer and the single family home is the "American Dream".

The "sensitives" are suspect of the future. Well-known is Orwell's **1984.** Popular movies written by "sensitives" that have touched the subconscious concern within the mass mind of the public are "Logan's Run", "Star Wars", and "Westworld". Movies that help Americans regress to more pleasant times are represented by the award winning movie, "The Sting".

America has had its share of prophets, but they have received little attention. Most accepted prophecy is tied to the **Bible,** and is concentrated in the book of Revelation. Many fundamental Christians believe these are the "end times". It is important to look at the Biblical evidence. Hal Lindsey's **The Late Great Planet Earth** is must reading in this regard. But Christians have thought it was the "end times" before. And they were wrong. Specifically, they were incorrect in Thessalonica as they were when the key year 1000 A.D. rolled around, in spite of the fact that an Ecumenical Council of the Roman Church had so declared 1000 A.D. as the "end times". A hundred years after Paul warned the Thessalonians against such folly, Montanus, a Christian zealot of central Turkey, again seduced Christians into believing the "end times" were at hand. In the fifth century, when Rome was sacked by Aryan Vandals, many Christians were positive the "last days" were near. During the same era when Columbus discovered America, Savonarola preached in Florence, Italy that doomsday was nigh. Thomas Malthus, an Anglican clergyman got Christian folks all stirred up in 1798 when he published, "An Essay on the Principle of Population as It Affects the Future Improvement of Society". He said, in effect, population would increase faster than the food supply. Eventually, there would be no food, and folks would die. At the very least, his timing was off. Johann Bengel, a German Lutheran scholar, predicted the end would come on June 18, 1836. William Miller, a New York minister called for the end between March 21, 1843 and March 21, 1844. Miller's followers climbed to tree tops and tried to fly to heaven. It was wild.[2] The call for doom was also heard during World War I and World War II. Jesus himself said, ". . . for ye know neither the day nor the hour wherein the Son of man cometh."[3] It is dangerous for Christians to believe that the Lord will "bail them out" of trouble in the upcoming difficult years! How much better to prepare for the worst, and pray for the best.

The father of the United States, George Washington, was a prophet. During the Revolutionary War, in 1777, at Valley Forge, Washington told of his vision to Anthony Sherman, a young soldier. The vision was published by Wesley Bradshaw in The National Tribune, Vol. 4, No. 12, December, 1880. The part of Washington's vision that applies to the future is as follows:

"Again I heard the mysterious voice saying, 'Son of the Republic, look and learn.' At this, the dark, shadowy angel placed a trumpet to his mouth, and blew three distinct blasts; and taking water from the ocean, he sprinkled it upon Europe, Asia and Africa.

Then my eyes beheld a fearful scene. From each of these continents arose thick black clouds that were soon joined into one. And throughout this mass there gleamed a dark-red light by which I saw hordes of armed men. These men, moving with the cloud, marched by land and sailed by sea to America, which country was enveloped in the volume of cloud. And I dimly saw these vast armies devastate the whole country and burn the villages, towns and cities, which I had seen springing up.

As my ears listened to the thundering of the cannon, clashing of swords, and the shouts and cries of millions in mortal combat, I again heard the mysterious voice saying, 'Son of the Republic, look and learn.' . . . As the voice ceased, the shadowy angel for the last time dipped water from the ocean and sprinkled it upon America. Instantly the dark cloud rolled back, together with the armies it had brought, leaving the inhabitants of the land victorious.

Then once more I beheld the villages, towns, and cities springing up where I had seen them before; while the bright angel, planting the azure Standard he had brought in the midst of them, cried in a loud voice: 'While the stars remain, and the heavens send down dew upon the earth, so long shall the Union last.' And taking from his brow the crown on which was blazoned the word, 'Union' he placed it upon the Standard while the people, kneeling down said, 'Amen!'

The scene instantly began to fade and dissolve, and I, at last saw nothing but the rising, curling vapor I at first beheld. This also disappeared, and I found myself once more gazing upon the mysterious visitor, who, in the same voice I had heard before, said, 'Son of the Republic, what you have seen is thus interpreted. Three great perils will come upon the Republic. The most fearful for her is the third. But the whole world united shall not prevail against her. Let every child of the Republic learn to live for his God, his land and Union.' With these words the vision vanished, and I started from my seat and felt that I had seen a vision wherein had been shown me the birth, the progress, and destiny of the United States."[4]

Charles David Evans, a Bishop of the Salem Ward, Palmyra Stake, Utah County, Utah, had a vision similar to Washington's on the evening of December 25, 1882. In his vision Evans saw a lust for power and money by those in positions of authority led to anarchy and violence throughout the United States. Bloodshed was widespread. After much hate, death, and anguish, men fought their way to power who believed in the original United States Constitution.[5]

Astrology also warns about the upcoming period. D. Modin, in his book, **Prophecy 1973-2000** states,

"In the Aquarian Age chart set for Washington, D.C. and progressing to 1976, Mars is coming to a conjunction of the Midheaven and is complete in 1983. This aspect is helping to reinforce the possibility of our involvement in a major global war.

In our progressed chart for 1982 our Sun is in Aquarius in the eleventh house with Mars in Libra, Neptune in Virgo in our seventh house, so with the rest of the conditions shown, we could fall into inner conflict and turmoil at that time, leaving the United States without a Federal Government. There could be an invasion from outside our continental boundaries. This is the time that we could be 'fighting in the cornfields of Iowa.'

The United States and the United Kingdom work as a unit and can be considered as one. Russia, China, and the United States, then, are the great powers that could wage global war. The most dangerous period, when such a war is most likely, is from 1976 to 1983."[6]

Additionally, Modin had his own vision of the future in 1946, while in British Columbia. Modin for some thirty years was a student of all kinds of prophecies. His studies included **The Four Vedas Sacred Sanscrits**, the **Bhagavad-Gita**, the **Shastra Bibles**, the **Zend-Avesta**, the **Sepher Bereshith Scriptures**, the **Kabala**, the **Talmud**, the **Tibetan Book of the Dead**, the **Egyptian Bible**, the **Weh of Cloth**, the **Koran,** the **Pentateuch,** the **Old Testament,** and the **Christian Bible.** His vision is as follows:

"I saw a new World War break out in the Pacific, its center in the Philippines. From there, it spread to encircle the world. I saw on one side the Christian forces, and on the other side the Buddhist and Mohammedan forces. Throughout the world, I saw destruction of the land, industry at a standstill, and people being killed almost instantly, on a massive scale. I saw the people of a new faith in the Far East looking to Palestine for safety.

Then the war between the nations stopped, and I saw revolution in each of the nations and great natural upheavals, the intent of which seemed to help break up the old conditions.

I saw the International Boundary at Blaine, Washington torn up clear across to Nova Scotia, where it disappeared. The American and Canadian governments broke up in chaos. I saw race rioting upon the American Continent on a vast scale. I saw hunger and disease throughout the world. Strife and chaos swept away the world we know. It was my impression that from the start of the Third World War this was all a continuous panorama, with different stages of development appearing simultaneously. First, world conflagration, then the break-down of national governments, followed by starvation, disease, and natural disasters. Then the scene ended."[7]

Chapter XII

W.D. Gann, The Master Forecaster

W.D. Gann is a market legend today, as he was in his own time. He was a genius who was held in awe by the lesser stock and commodity traders during the first half of this century. Thought by many to be arrogant and proud, Gann simply exhibited the self-confidence that comes from wisdom, knowledge, and understanding. It is a power only understood by those who possess it.

Gann's genius was confirmed by the fact that over 85% of his predictions over many years were correct. For fifty years he was a dominating figure in the American marketplace. He was called "The Authority on Predictions of Securities," "The Guru of Wall Street," and "The Master Economic Forecaster."

Gann pulled in excess of $50 million from the stock and commodity markets over a fifty year period (uninflated dollars). He knew well ahead of time exactly what the markets would do. He was a man far ahead of his time then, and probably now. If ever a man understood the relationships between time and price, human action, and the relationships between planetary forces and economic events, it was W.D. Gann. He understood secrets of the universe that lie undiscovered today. His often so-called contempt for his fellow man was not the result of his personal pride, but rather the opposite. Gann knew that man was nothing, insignificant in the face of the God of the universe and His natural laws. (Gann's last book was entitled, **The Magic Word, Jehovah.**) It was his humility, his sense of submission to the laws of the universe that made Gann great, as well as rich.

Gann studied, really studied. His charts and other work on markets literally fill a moving van. It is doubtful that the work of ten men, working all their lives, could equal his production. Some commodities he researched back four centuries in order to learn their natural cycles. He was a profilic writer. His books include **Profits in Commodities, 45 Years in Wall Street, Truth of the Stock Tape,** and **How to Make Money in Puts and Calls.**

Gann explained his success.

"I figure things by mathematics. There is nothing mysterious about any of my predictions. If I have the data, I can use algebra and geometry and tell exactly by the theory of cycles when a certain thing is going to occur again.

If we wish to avert failure in speculation, we must deal with causes Everything in existence is based on exact proportion and perfect relationship. There is no chance in nature, because mathematic principles of the highest order lie at the foundation of all things. Faraday said: 'There is nothing in the universe but mathematical points of force.' "[1]

Gann practiced what he preached. His old charts are loaded with time and price clocks for all commodities. Who can argue with a man who is 85% percent correct and makes $50 million? Are the relativists listening?

Gann was much more than just a student of the markets. His charts and his library reveal a wealth of wisdom. No one knows for sure how much Gann learned from the Tibetan monks about the ancient mystery schools, and how this experience affected his trading and understanding.

Gann correctly called his own year of death - 1956. But he also peered into the future to see what was ahead. Among Gann's old torn and dusty papers are his "war charts." These were Gann's deepest secret. He researched battles among people that most historians don't even know existed. Listed on his "War-Battles, Time Periods in Years Between Decisive Battles" are notations such as the following:

"Greco-Persian - 499-478 B.C., Athens-Sparta - 431-404 B.C., Macedonia-Persia 334-323 B.C., Alexander Succession & Samnite - 323-280 B.C., Punic Wars, Rome vs. Carthage, Gallic Wars - 58-51 B.C., Roman Civil Wars - 50-45 B.C., 43-42 B.C., 31-30 B.C., Teutons vs. Romans - 9 A.D., Conquest of Britain 43 - 85 A.D., Western Roman - 312 A.D., Vandals - 402 - 455 A.D., Moors vs. Visigoths 711 - 732 A.D., Conquest of England - 1066 A.D., Seven Crusades & Children's Crusade - 11th & 13th Century, Hundred Years War - 1337 - 1453, War of Roses - 1455 - 1485, Spanish Armada - 1588, Thirty-Years War - 1618-1648, Gt. Rebellion - 1642 - 1652, Spanish Succession - 1701 - 1714, Austrian Succession 1740 - 1748, Seven Years War - 1756 - 1763, American Revolution - 1775 - 1783, French Revolution - 1789 - 1799, Napoleonic Wars - 1796 - 1815, War of 1812 - 1812, Mexican War - 1846 - 1848, Crimean War - 1854 - 1856, Civil War - 1861 - 1865, Seven Weeks War - 1866, Franco - Prussian - 1870 - 1871, Chinese - Japanese - 1894 - 1895, Spanish-American - 1898, Boer - War - 1899 - 1902." [2]

These are just a few of the wars that Gann studied. One gets the idea that Gann knew quite a bit about war. One also gets the impression that war is a pretty regular occurrence in the affairs of men.

In 1914, Gann predicted World War I. In March of 1918, he called for the end of the war and the Kaiser's abdication. The prediction was commented on by **The Houston Post** and the **New York Herald.** In July of 1939, he predicted the beginning of World War II.

On April 5, 1954, Gann wrote,

"After fifty-two years of experience and research going back hundreds of years, I have proven to my entire satisfaction that history repeats and that when we know the past, we can determine the future of prices. I put TIME CYCLES to the test in my personal trading, and I have issued Annual Forecasts on Stocks and Commodities for more than 50 years which have proven accurate.

TIME CYCLES repeat because human nature does not change. That is why wars occur at regular CYCLES . . . ."[3]

Gann passed from this earth in 1956. His war charts saw Viet Nam. They also predict war in 1982-83. Who is willing to bet against W.D. Gann?

Chapter XIII

Cycles of War and Caesar

It is time to regroup and summarize the evidence that indicates that both internal strife and international war are a probability during the next six years.

1. Dr. McClelland's study of American literature indicates that the American people are psychologically inclined for war on a scale not seen since 1825. Dr. Billy Graham confirmed with the studies of a Western European psychiatrist. Lloyd deMause also confirmed.

2. Brinton's studies on how the potential or approaching bankruptcy of government foreshadows internal strife, as does inflation, as covered by **London Times** editor, William Rees-Mogg, and Nobel Prize winner, F.A. Hayek, were discussed. Additionally, the United States scored highly on 6 of the 7 other points Brinton mentioned that precede revolution. L.J. Jensen's work with planets, business cycles, monetary instability, and political unrest as forecast for the upcoming 1980 period was reviewed and confirmed by David Williams. Also, Jack Sauers' thoughts on the gold standard and revolution in the near future were covered.

3. The work of Winkless and Browning on how the coming cooler and harsher climate would make man more warlike was discussed, as well as the 800-year cycle, the 45-year cycle, and its implications for drought and

depression. Dr. Wheeler's work on the 100-year cycle in climatic conditions, and the present Cold-Dry period, was discussed in light of its potential for race riots, revolutions, and migrations. The Drought and Civil War Clock was presented. Dewey's 142-year cycle, 57-year cycle, and cyclical Index of International Battles confirmed the potential for war in the next six years. The problems associated with the 1982 "Jupiter Effect," and the peak of the 11-year sunspot cycle were discussed. Also, the evidence concerning the possibility of a polar shift was mentioned.

4. Governmental interference with free markets was shown to be a cause of war, and protectionism on a national level now is becoming widespread. The resource crises in water, food, and energy, were revealed to be problems that could well lead to violent conflict. The way a market tops out was compared to overpopulation vs. resource demands, and the natural adjustment of reduced population via war was discussed.

5. The conclusions of the respected historians, Toynbee, Spengler, and Riencourt, were brought out to air and shown to be in conformity - a time of trouble, war, and strife is near.

6. The susceptibility of the cities in time of crisis and the resultant violence was brought to light in the words of Roberto Vacca, Paul Popenoe, Gibson Winter, Margaret Mead, J.D. Unwin, and Howard J. Ruff.

7. Hutner's Cycle of Optimism and Pessimism, the 50-year cycles, and the lesser business cycles were contrasted with the expectations of the minorities and shown to hold the seeds of unrest and violent conflict.

8. The Kondratieff Cycle was reviewed in light of the potential for a peak war and the violence associated with the equivalence of male and female.

9. The low level of the U.S. military's preparation for war was revealed to be a harbinger of war by Winkless and Browning, Will Rogers, The Collins Report, and A.P. writers Arnett and Hoffman. The probability for war was deemed likely by the Stockholm International Peace Research Institute.

10. The visions of George Washington, Charles David Evans, and D. Modin were ominous. Astrology predicts the next six years to be fraught with trouble and war. W. D. Gann confirms.

What does all the evidence forecast on a probabilistic basis? It forebodes a chaotic time in the near future when the way of life will bear no resemblance to the lifestyle known today. There is no future as is now known? As Winkless and Browning observed, "The course of history is not smooth, but occurs as a series of abrupt lurches and staggers with occasional periods of steadiness."[1]

Presently, the world is at peace. But as Oswald Spengler stated in **The Decline of the West,**

"... *world-peace - which has often existed in fact - involves the private renunciation of war on the part of the immense majority, but along with this, it involves an unavowed readiness to submit to being the booty of others who do not renounce it. It begins with the state-destroying wish for universal reconciliation, and it ends in nobody's moving a finger so long as misfortune only touches his neighbor.*"[2]

Written in the 1920's Spengler correctly projected the progression of communism since World War II.

The United States democracy is thriving on one man, one vote. But as John Adams warned his countrymen in 1815, "Democracy has never been and never can be so desirable as aristocracy or monarchy, but while it lasts, is more bloody than either. Remember, democracy never lasts long. It soon wastes, exhausts, and murders itself. There never was a democracy that did not commit suicide."[3] Alexander Hamilton said: "We are a Republic. Real liberty is never found in despotism or in the extremes of democracy."[4] James Madison stated, "Democracies have ever been spectacles of turbulence and contention; have ever been found incompatible with personal security, or the rights of property; and have been as short in their lives as they have been violent in their deaths."[5] John Marshall, Chief Justice of the Supreme Court, declared, "Between a balanced republic and a democracy, the difference is like that between order and chaos."[6]

Should a major crisis eventuate, such as a war, the call will be for instant action and strong leadership. The more grave the crisis, the more the American people have looked to their President for leadership. (Fire brigades are not formed or run by committees.) And the President has traditionally responded in a dictatorial fashion, usurping powers not given him by the constitution. Also, his actions have historically been applauded by the American people.

For example, in 1864, Lincoln permitted fraudulent elections in order to insure his retention of power.

"He condoned unconstitutional pressure on the wavering border states . . . . He suspended the writ of habeas corpus over the protests of the Chief Justice, asked for troops without legal authority, started the war before calling Congress in 1861, built a national army instead of relying on local militias, issued his Emancipation Proclamations in 1862 and 1863 without previous legislative sanction, ... His virtual dictatorship was based on a sober but ruthless idealism which, once in action, stopped at nothing . . . .

. . . . As Lincoln's Secretary of State put it to a British correspondent, 'We elect a king for

four years and give him absolute powers within certain limits, which, after all, he can interpret for himself.' "[7]

Andrew Jackson had increased the concentration of power in the White House. "King Andrew", as his enemies called him, stated that only the President is "the direct representative of the people, and responsible to them." Of the Senate he stated, "a body not directly amenable to the people." Jackson vetoed so many bills that Henry Clay remarked,

" 'Really, and in practice, the veto power drew after it the power of initiating laws, and in its effects must ultimately amount to conferring on the executive the entire legislative power to consummate legislation, to give vitality and vigor to every law or to strike it dead at his pleasure, the President must ultimately become the ruler of the nation . . . . The government will have been transformed into an elective monarch."[8]

Franklin D. Roosevelt's powers were such that American historian, W. Binkley, stated, " 'In truth, the office of the President has been altered beyond recognition as Mr. Roosevelt exercised the powers of a dictator.' "[9] Americans fully accepted the concentration of power in Roosevelt's hands. In the campaign of 1940, in a speech in Cleveland, Ohio when Roosevelt stated that when the next four years were over, "There will be another President," the crowd shouted, NO! NO! Quick of mind, Roosevelt continued talking close to the microphone so that those listening on the radio would not hear the shouts that suggested he be elected permanently.[10]

Much has been written about the fall of Rome, and how it compares with the United States. Two excellent works on the subject are Edward Gibbon's, **The Decline and Fall of the Roman Empire,** and Amaury de Riencourt's, **The Coming Caesars.** Under what conditions can a Caesar come to Power?

For purposes here, the topic shall be explored under the following headings: General Comments, Historical Development, Parallels in Rome's Rise to Caesarism, and America Today.

General Comments

The natural progression of events is from a growing democracy to imperialism. Imperialism destroys the earlier republican institutions. Social equality comes to the fore, and liberty lessens as the society becomes more egalitarian. With the egalitarian tendency, increasing power accrues in the hands of one man. What is often not understood about Caesarism is that it is not a dictatorship, nor a clandestine grasp of power. Caesarism is demanded by the people. Caesar is loved, and is welcome in almost all homes for dinner and a fireside chat. It is the result of a natural progression by a free people who no longer desire the responsibilities of freedom, and thus turn it over to one man. The road to Caesarism is a practical one, a pragmatic one. It is an escape from freedom.

Freedom is not compatible with security. Security can best be maximized in a jail cell (maximum security) or in a hospital. Freedom entails the assumption of risk. The tendency of Americans to look to the government for job security, Social Security, etc., speaks for itself. It is evidence of a desire to avoid risk. Caesar provides security, and assumes the risk.

Also, as has been witnessed by many political observers in the 1970's, democratic governments are failing badly at handling international affairs. Therefore, for all practical matters, foreign policy is set by the White House, the logical seat of approaching Caesarism. The "liberal" leaders in their promotion of big government, are unconsciously taking the United States not to the left, but to the right, where an autocratic master will prevail. The country has almost made a complete cycle back to the point from which the American Revolution began - a revolution for liberty against oppressive monarchs, and unfair taxation. Indeed, the growing tax revolt movement in the United States is a response to the oppression of taxes and the tyranny of the Internal Revenue Service.

Historical Development

From earlier quotes, it is obvious that the founders of the republic of the United States had no confidence whatsoever in one man, one vote - democracy. The true liberals who wrote the Articles of Confederation were additionally convinced that democracy was impossible, as well as impractical, under a centralized government ruling over a large geographic area. Their fear was that such a situation would evolve into a despicable monarchy.

Leaders such as Locke, John Jay, James Madison, and Alexander Hamilton took a strong stand for limited government. Locke saw government's primary function to be the protection of private property. These men believed in the **inequality** of man, and they saw the greatest threat to liberty to be in equality. That equality is the emphasis of the federal government deserves no argument. Undoubtedly, the early leaders never dreamed the Presidency would be transformed into the Tribune of the People that it is today. The founding fathers were conservative. They went to great pains to prevent democracy through the Constitution.

Political parties were another anathema to the founding fathers. It was one of the four major dangers warned against by Washington in his farewell address. But it was the split between Jefferson and Hamilton which gave birth to what the founding fathers had always wanted to avoid - political parties. They had written a constitution which seemed to preclude political parties. A final attempt to rule without political parties was carried out by John Quincy Adams. It lead to a deadlock.

As can be the case, when the traditional ruling classes falter, democracy can fill the void. Politics then becomes a business, run by professionals. A rise in the standard of living only complicates matters. The new rich look down on politics as a dirty affair to be manipulated in the interest of business.

As early as 1800, influential Easterners saw that sooner or later, Caesarism would come to America. The rise to power of Andrew Jackson marked a clean turn when U.S. voters stopped focusing on issues, and instead focused on individuals. Speaking of the era of Andrew Jackson, historian Alexis de Tocqueville commented,

> " 'It has been imagined that General Jackson is bent on establishing a dictatorship in America, introducing a military spirit, and giving a degree of influence to the central authority that cannot but be dangerous to provincial liberty . . . but in America, the time for similar undertakings in the age for men of this kind, has not yet come.' "[11]

Tocqueville saw all too clearly that such a day **would come.** Professional political machines prevailed in the days of Jackson. Americans were glad to avoid the bother. There was no ruling leisured class or gentry to oppose the professionals.

It was under Franklin D. Roosevelt, which was the last time that America faced a major crisis, that the escape from freedom and commensurate responsibility and authority became openly and clearly evident. The Welfare State, under the all powerful paternalistic state, provided the desired security. The difficulty experienced by the average man in attempting to deal with the size and complexity of society became too great. He acquiesced to the centuries old cycle of surrending freedom for economic protection.

Parallels in Rome's Rise to Caesarism

Rome stressed conformity. So does the United States. The American dream of owning "my own home", and the standardization of single family dwellings, is constantly remarked upon by foreign visitors. Romans had highly standardized names. So do Americans. In the telephone directory of major cities, one need only to check the incredible number of Bobs, Jims, Johns, Franks, Davids, and Toms to confirm the collective tendency. The mass production of the public school system and state supported universities are another easy example. Subject matter is, for all practical matters, identical. Team athletics are stressed. Higher education emphasizes training to "fit the system," just as it did in Rome. (By contrast, Greece promoted the full development of individual idiosyncrasies.) Not since Rome has the world seen such an incredible striving for identical life styles. In Rome and in America, religious tension between ruthless materialism and idealism existed. Both civilizations emphasized the rule of law.

America Today

Americans today distrust the Congress. Their natural impatience with the lethargy of that august body breeds contempt. Americans are emotional and are hero worshippers. They are used to bosses and regimentation in their daily lives. They are conditioned by sophisticated transportation systems, and governmental and corporate bureaucracies, not to mention the indoctrination by the standarized mass media. The effectiveness of mass advertising is a case in point.

Americans are gregarious. The number of leagues, councils, associations, committees, fraternities, clubs,

Chambers of Commerce, societies, and lodges is truly amazing. Americans as joiners are willing to follow a leader. A tally of the small groups of men who wield power in business and politics is evidence of this.

The United States today is a Civilization, the prelude to a Caesar. The United States has intensive corporate agriculture, large populations packed together in cities, sophisticated and efficient systems of distributions, occupational specialization, different social classes, and a pervasive central government - all characteristics of a Civilization. When do Civilizations fail, and open the door for Caesar? According to Voltaire, it is when a nation gets too luxurious, soft, and successful. It was Louis Wallis' conviction in **An Examination of Society,** that Civilizations fail when there is a vast concentration of land holdings, which has a negative effect on morale and morals. According to Eric Fischer (**The Passing of the European Age**), it is when the culture fails to adapt to new conditions. Tom B. Jones' work, **Ancient Civilization,** held that collapse came when raw materials were used up at home, and then imported until they could no longer be afforded. **The Law of Civilization and Decay** by Brooks Adams stated the decline came when there was a concentration of power and decision making in the hands of a few. In **Family and Civilization,** Dr. Carle C. Zimmerman stated the demise of Civilization was due to the demise of the family. Howard H. Smith in the January 8, 1955, **Saturday Review,** stated it was due to exploding knowledge, and increased complexity that resulted in each generation knowing less per individual of the total cultural heritage than the generation that went before it. W.B. Pitkin argued that the fall comes when an overwhelming population hinders individual initiative and achievement.[12] Elmer Pendell, in **Why Civilizations Self-Destruct,** stated time was up when the less capable members of the society outbreed the more capable.[13] He stated, "There is no deadlier form of self-destruction than forcing the worthy elements of a Civilization to become the servants of the drones."[14]

The point is this. Any of the above conditions for failure apply to the United States today in varying degrees. Thus, any of a number of crises could usher in the era of Caesar.

And there is yet another. Toward the end of the Hellenistic Age, there was no greater revolution in Rome than that of women's rights. In the Second Century B.C., they became emancipated in every way, including economically. The United States' declaration that all men are created equal in terms of practical ability excluded women. Apparently, the difference in essence was enough. The growing role of women in the United States has led to many changes in public opinion, including the following: the desire for freedom to be replaced by security, the tendency to focus on the child, and the youth worship syndrome, the suspicion of individualism, the desire to avoid risk, and the emotional personalization of issues. In Rome, the increasing voice of women in formulating public opinion resulted in the establishment of a virile Caesar. Masses of people, such as are found in the cities of the United States today, display the emotionalism collectively that is common to women. They must instinctively look for compensating masculine leadership, which cannot be found in a congress, but in a Caesar.

Today, the climate is right for the rise of Caesar. All that is needed is a crisis demanding immediate decisions. The powers are already established in the Presidency. The President has Executive Orders to be used in an emergency. He is head of the country, the Tribune of the People, the dictator of foreign policy, master legislator, the head of his party, keeper of the economy, leader of western civilization, and Commander-in-Chief of the Armed Forces.

Rome learned in the Punic and Macedonian Wars that crises in an equalitarian society demand a Caesar. The Romans discovered that in such emergencies responsibility must be located in one man, not a congress. Grave emergencies do not allow the time for discussion, argument and voting. The world finds itself today in a state of permanent emergency. Such states give rise to Caesar. Wars are the primary forerunners of Caesarism.

It could be argued that the U.S. constitutional system of checks and balances is the last stand against the rise of Caesarism. Critics could point to Richard Nixon as a case in point of how abuse of power was rightly checked. It must be remembered, however, that the United States was not in a state of emergency during the Nixon/Watergate crisis, not the type of crisis, at least, that requires instant decisions as does a war.

Congress is presently abdicating its remaining legislative powers to the President. As Alan L. Otten declared in the August 18, 1977, issue of the **Wall Street Journal** in an article entitled, "Errand Boys.",

"The newer Congressmen don't care too much about shaping major government policies and programs. They seem far more interested in simply running errands for their constituents.

That, at least, is the conclusion of a good many veteran lawmakers, lobbyists, and others who've watched the horde of Democrats elected to the House of Representatives in 1976 and 1977.

. . . . this devotion to casework and downplaying of policy will continue. Most lawmakers, new and old, are inclined to agree.

'Once you start down the road,' observes a

thoughtful GOP Congressman, 'once you establish that kind of pattern here, you don't change very easily.'

. . . . in this day of public alienation from government . . . acting as a buffer between the frustrated citizen and frustrating bureaucrat - may actually be a Congressman's most important job."[15]

The prolific writer and economist, Dr. Gary North, worked in Washington for some time on the staff of Congressman Ron Paul from Houston, Texas. He wrote of his experiences in the August 19, 1977 issue of **Remnant Review,** in an article cleverly entitled, "Confessions of a Washington Reject." Dr. North comments,

". . . people with principles get eaten up and spit out by this system. How to manage 200 pages of **Congressional Record** *every day, plus the hearings in committee, plus the* **Federal Register,** *plus the speeches on the road, plus the party (political organization) pressures, plus the party (riotous escape) pressures? No one can do it. No group can do it. The dreams of messianic legislation and comprehensive political predestination have not come to heavenly fruition, but they have driven mad those who had such visions. The pursuit of total planning has eaten up the legislators in the last 15 years. They are retiring in droves. Something like 50% of the men in the House today weren't there in the late 1960's . . . . The whole system is collapsing, and both the conservatives and ideological liberals know it, but the conservatives can't do anything about it, and the liberals won't do anything about it. They are caught on a sort of demonic treadmill to legislative oblivion."*[16]

Speaking of the Congressional staffs, North wrote,

"Seldom in the history of man have so many in-

competents, cronies, idiots, goof-offs, hangers-on, and nincompoops been assembled in one geographical area. The mediocrity of the Congressional staffs is, above all, the fact that struck me hardest. Grafters are to be expected in government, but these people are yo-yos . . . . What goes wrong? It's a complicated problem. Here is my evaluation. **First,** *Congressmen don't want to hire people smarter than they are. This reduces the level of competence to levels undreamed of.* **Second,** *they don't hire anyone anyway. Their administrative assistants do the hiring . . . ."*[17]

Dr. North's most sobering comments were with regard to where the legislation comes from. The shadow of Caesar is growing.

". . . I'll tell you one thing: the office staffs don't create the prominent laws that get the headlines and cost the billions. The executive has tremendous influence in this area, and I suspect that it is through the executive bureaucratic staffs that significant batches of the legislation get submitted to Congress. This is where the think-tanks like Brookings Institution get the ball rolling. Congress is an uncreative institution today."[18]

Chapter XIV

The Powerful Elite

Dr. Gary North in his August 18, 1976 **Remnant Review** observed that the **Federal Register,** the law of the land, contains 60,000 pages a year, which no Congressman has time to read. He stated, ". . . We have seen the fruition of the prophecy made by F.A. Hayek in his 1944 book, **The Road to Serfdom:** the triumph of elitist bureaucrats in the name of participatory democracy. Congress cannot plan Congress, let alone the whole economy."[1]

The **Federal Register** includes Executive Orders, 12,000 of them. One of the most frightening of them is Executive Order 11921, issued as Part IV of the **Federal Register,** Vol. 41, No. 116 (June 15, 1976). North commented, "How bad is the latest Executive Order? Very very, bad. Mindbogglingly bad . . . . The day of the Caesar is already on the statute books. It only awaits a set of circumstances including a risk-oriented President, to inaugurate that day."[2] It is interesting to reflect upon the fact that Mr. Carter is a self-made millionaire - a risk taker. Remember the dangerous rapids Burt Reynolds ran in the movie, "Deliverance"? Mr. Carter shot them too.

Executive Order 11921 permits the following: (1) Total government censorship, (2) The production and distribution of all materials, (3) The use of all production facilities, (4) Production, and distribution of, and the use of facilities for petroleum, solid fuels, gas, electric power, water, food, farm equipment, fertilizer, and minerals, (5) Domestic distribution of health resources, (6) Construction, use, and management of highways, streets, appurtenant structures, and civil aviation facilities, and that's just a starter. In other words, total government control is the goal.[3] All it takes to trigger this Order is an emergency, such as a war.

Howard J. Ruff, in his August, 1, 1977, **Ruff Times** brings to light Executive Order 11921. Ruff states, "If you read this 35-page Executive Order carefully, you will realize that it gives the President absolutely dictatorial powers."[4] The Order can be put into effect by the President "in any national emergency type situation that might conceivably confront the nation." The President, among other things, has the power to take control of all emergency sources. Under his direction, the departments of government can develop wage and price controls, freeze money in banks, seize and dispose of real and personal property, close security exchanges and prevent capital from leaving the country, plus more.[5]

In view of the fact that the United States has accelerated on the road to Caesarism, and the Executive Orders provide the power for implementation, it is important to look at the power block that brought Mr. Carter to office, for therein lies the influence on the Executive.

The "radical fringe" has long promoted a conspiracy theory of power. For our purposes, only publications of accepted reputation will be examined. First, a perusal of an article in the April 1977 issue of **Reason** magazine, the publication of the intellectuals, and then a look at the July 1977 issue of **The Atlantic Monthly,** the magazine of the eastern financial elite, is in order.

Murray N. Rothbard, Professor of Economics at The Polytechnic Institute of New York, reasons in an article entitled, "The Conspiracy Theory of History Revisited,", in **Reason** magazine. He states,

"Anytime that a hard-nosed analysis is put forth of who our rulers are, of how their political and economic interests interlock, it is invariably denounced by Establishment liberals and conservatives as a 'conspiracy theory of history', 'paranoid,' 'economic determinist,' and even 'Marxist.' These smear labels are applied across the board, even though such realistic analyses can be, and have been, made from any and all parts of the economic spectrum, from John Birch Society to the Communist Party . . . .

It is no wonder that usually these realistic analyses are spelled out by various 'extremists' who are outside the Establishment consensus. For it is vital to the continued rule of the State apparatus that it have legitimacy and even sanctity in the eyes of the public; and it is vital to that sanctity that our politicians and bureaucrats be deemed to be disembodied spirits solely devoted to the public good. Once let the cat out of the bag that these spirits are all too often grounded in the solid earth of advancing a set of economic interests through use of the State, and the basic mystique of government begins to collapse."[6]

Dr. Rothbard goes on to comment that the conspiracy analyst is a realist in the sense that the conspiracy analyst believe folks tend to act in their own self-interest, and that the use of government can be a very helpful means to achieving one's ends. It is naive to believe that a series of events in government, ". . . are random and unplanned, and that therefore people do not engage in purposive choice and planning."[7]

Dr. Rothbard notes, for a case in point, that even the major newsweeklies have commented on the fact that almost all the top leadership in Mr. Carter's administration are members of the elite Trilateral Commission, which was founded by David Rockefeller in 1973. The purpose of the Trilateral Commission is to formulate policies in the unified best interest of the United States, Japan, and Western Europe, ". . . and/or members of the board of the Rockefeller Foundation."[8] Mr. Carter, Mondale, and important members of the Coca-Cola Company, Georgia's largest corporation, are all members of the Trilateral Commission.

Dr. Rothbard thinks it is foolish to believe ". . . that David Rockefeller's prodigious efforts on behalf of certain statist public policies are merely a reflection of unfocused altruism."[9] It makes more sense to assume that economic interest was at stake. Professor Rothbard concludes,

". . . Was Jimmy Carter named a member of the Trilateral Commission as soon as it was founded because Rockefeller and others wanted to hear the wisdom of an obscure Georgia governor? Or was he plucked out of obscurity and made President by their support? Was J. Paul Austin, head of Coca-Cola, an early supporter of Jimmy Carter merely out of concern for the common good? Were all the Trilateralists and Rockefeller Foundation and Coca-Cola people chosen by Carter simply because he felt that they were the ablest possible people for the job? If so, it's a coincidence that boggles the mind. Or are there more sinister political-economic interests involved? I submit that the naifs who stubbornly refuse to examine the interplay of political and economic interest in government are tossing away an essential tool for analyzing the world in which we live."[10]

The July 1977 **Atlantic Monthly** lends credibility to Professor Rothbard's remarks in articles entitled, "Carter Revealed: He's a Rockefeller Republican," and "The Trilateral Connection." It's all there, David Rockefeller's brain child - The Trilateral Commission, **Time** magazine's support of Mr. Carter throughout his campaign, how

Zbigniew Brzezinski, full-time director of the Trilateral Commission, was Mr. Carter's tutor, and how Rockefeller tied into the Southern black community through King's Southern Leadership Conference. The author, Christopher Lydon, further states that other than the Trilateral Commission, the only person who could claim a piece of Mr. Carter's presidency was Andrew Young, now U.N. Ambassador. Lydon believes Mr. Carter has used modern communications to a degree of effectiveness never achieved before.

"... *Jimmy Carter has refined the imperial tricks of the electronic age, detaching the presidency from popular direction, and the old institutional restraints. The brilliant devices of his in-office campaign to stay close to the people serve the imperial purpose, of course. The 'dial-the-president' lottery that gives every phone caller the same chance of talking to President Carter and Walter Cronkite is a nice way of saying that there is no one that Jimmy Carter has to talk to. All citizens, all power centers, are equidistant from this President, who wants to be close to everyone.*"[11]

Lydon notes that "... Robert Shurn, a disillusioned liberal speech writer, ... quit Carter's campaign staff with the observation to the candidate, 'I am not sure what you truly believe in other than yourself.' "[12]

The second article in this back to back **Atlantic Monthly** series is even more shocking. It is entitled "The Trilateral Connection", written by Jeremiah Novak. Novak states, "For the third time in this century, a group of American scholars, businessmen, and government officials are planning to fashion a new world order."[13] The purpose of The Trilateral Commission is to have a community of developed nations to coordinate international, economic, and political affairs. Sixteen (16) of Mr.

Carter's appointees are members of the Commission.[14] They include the following:

1. Zbigniew Brzezinski, National Security Advisor
2. Cyrus Vance, Secretary of State
3. Walter Mondale, Vice President
4. W. Michael Blumenthal, Secretary of Treasury
5. Harold Brown, Secretary of Defense
6. Richard Holbrooke, Assistant Secretary for East Asian and Pacific Affairs
7. Warren Christopher, Deputy Secretary of State
8. Richard N. Cooper, Under Secretary of State for Economic Affairs
9. Andrew Young, U.S. Ambassador to the United States
10. C. Fred Bergsten, Assistant Secretary of the Treasury for Int'l Economic Affairs

The Trilateral Commission has provided the following advisors for Mr. Carter.

1. Lane Kirkland, Secretary - Treasurer of AFL-CIO
2. Henry Owens, Director of Foreign Policy Studies Program, The Brookings Institution
3. Leonard Woodcock, President of United Automobile Workers
4. Robert Roosa, partner with Brown Brothers
5. J. Paul Austin, Chairman of Coca-Cola Company[15]

Isn't it interesting that Bert Lance is not a member of this elite group? Isn't it strange that Mr. Lance is no longer part of Mr. Carter's team?

The sixteen men all represent a ". . . deeply internationalist tradition that is part of the Eastern American establishment . . . . 'Liberal internationalism is our creed,' said Fred Bergsten, Asst. Secretary of Treasury, 'and Jimmy Carter is its prophet.' "[16] Mr. Carter, as a charter member of The Trilateral Commission, advocates its basic internationalist viewpoint?

"If there is one book in Carter's gospel, it is Zbigniew Brzezinski's, **Between Two Ages,** *published in 1970, in which Brzezinski, now National Security Advisor, formed the concept of a 'community of developed nations' that would direct the world to new levels of freedom, human rights, and economic progress."*[17]

This community of developed nations included Western Europe, Japan, the United States, and other advanced nations including communist ones. (It is interesting to note that Brzezinski's message did not find acceptance until the United States went off the gold standard in December of 1971.) The Trilateral Commission pinpointed the vital political objective - to gain control of the American Presidency.[18] Clearly, it is out in the open - Eastern establishment intellectuals and Wall Street interests in collusion with government, controlling the most powerful political office in the world.

"For as Samuel Huntington, a Harvard government professor and a Trilateral scholar has written, 'To the extent that the United States was governed by anyone in the decades after World War Two, it was governed by the President.' "[19] Peter Boune, Mr. Carter's former Deputy Campaign Chief, has been quoted as saying that both David Rockefeller and Brzezinski had agreed that Mr. Carter was the ideal politician upon whom to build their base.[20] Perhaps that explains UPI correspondent Helen Thomas' quote of Mr. Carter. Mr. Carter stated, "I've chosen a cabinet, most of whom I did not know ahead of time, who are superb. There is not a single Cabinet member whom I consider to be weak or whom I would replace if I had free option to do so."[21] Mr. Carter is stating that he did not choose his cabinet, and more importantly, he did not know anything about them. Also, he can't fire them. The Ship of State is in elitist hands.

Novak continues,

"The Trilateralists emphasis on economics is not entirely disinterested, for the oil crisis forced many developing nations, with doubtful repayment abilities, to borrow excessively. All total, private multinational banks, particularly Rockefeller's Chase Manhattan, has loaned nearly $52 billion to developing countries. An overhauled IMF would provide another source of credit for these nations, and would take the big private banks off the hook."[22]

Big private banking, linked with big government, with the danger of an international money crisis, is revealed.

"To implement its aims, The Trilateral Commission has called for the formation of commissions to coordinate the political and economic power of the Trilateral areas. These commissions will subordinate national economic policy to international needs."[23]

Larry Spence, Penn State political scientist, criticized Samuel Huntington, editor of the voice of The Trilateral Commission's **Foreign Policy** magazine, when he stated, " 'If he (Huntington) gets his way, we will have a new supernational community dominated by the multinational corporations.' "[24] Some of the corporate executives who are Trilateralists include the executives of Bank of America, First National City Bank, Exxon, Caterpillar, CBS, Thyssen, Royal Dutch Petroleum, Unilever, Bank of Tokyo, and Fuji Bank. Novak concludes, "In the last analysis, it is Carter who directs the third try for a new world order."[25]

Finally, an article in a nonpolitical publication highlights the seriousness of the fact that the United States government is no longer of the people, by the people, or for the people. **Penthouse,** of all places, (November, 1977) featured an article by Craig S. Karpel entitled, "Cartergate: The Death of Democracy." Karpel states,

"The presidency of the United States and the key cabinet departments of the federal government have been taken over by a private organization dedicated to the subordination of the domestic interests of the United States to the international interests of the multi-national banks and corporations.

The seizure of public power by private interests is the most serious political scandal in American history . . . .

. . . . It would be unfair to say that The Trilateral Commission dominates the Carter administration. The Trilateral Commission is the Carter administration."[26]

Here too, the founding of The Trilateral Commission by David Rockefeller is discussed, along with Brzezinski's plan to unite the United States, West Germany, and Japan, ". . . into an alliance that would rule the world and exploit their own citizens."[27] The support given Mr. Carter by CBS, **Time, Inc.,** the **Chicago Sun-Times,** and the heavyweights of the **Wall Street Journal, New York Times,** and the **Los Angeles Times** is all there. Karpel notes that every major action by Mr. Carter has been in the best interest of The Trilateral Commission. He documents his case, point by point. One example was the May 1977 London Summit meeting. Its purpose was to convince Western Europe and Japan to,

". . . expand their economies even at the risk of hurting domestic industry, pay more of their tax-payers' money into the International Monetary Fund so that it could bail out Third World countries that are in danger of defaulting on huge loans from the U.S. banks represented on The Trilateral Commission, and force consumers to pay higher prices for Third World commodities so that the oil-fleeced, less-

developed countries could afford to pay back the billions they owe the New York banks . . . ."[28]

Karpel points out that the dollar devaluation is in the best interest of the multinationals because,

> *"First, they raise the prices of the products they sell in the United States so that they can pass through to the consumer the increased cost of imported raw materials. But labor contracts make it possible for them to delay raising wages proportionally . . . the wages that they're paying out never rise as fast as the prices they're taking in.*
>
> *Simultaneously, when the value of other currencies goes up compared with that of the dollar, the multinationals' balance sheets look better, because the foreign currency they're earning overseas is suddenly worth more in dollars. . . ."*[29]

Some $50 billion is owed to U.S. banks by the Third World countries. They cannot pay. Zaire recently defaulted. The banks cannot repossess a country. If a domino effect ensues, with other less-developed countries defaulting on their loans, the banking system collapses. Karpel states The Trilateral solution:

> *"The only solution is to lend the deadbeat LDC's still more money to pay off the loans that are about to go sour. Problem: the banks don't have enough good money to throw after bad - because they have already lent all the good money to the LDC's that now can't pay. Solution: steal the money from the U.S. tax-payer."*[30]

The banks in trouble are the giants - Chase Manhattan, Citibank, Bank of America, Morgan Guaranty Trust, and First National Bank of Chicago, just to mention a few. A crisis in one of these monsters could trigger a "run" on the banks.

With regard to the "human rights" issue, Karpel declares, "The real purpose of the human rights issue is to put a politically popular veneer of morality on an American foreign policy based purely on economic considerations . . . ."[31] He discusses how Mr. Carter worked behind the scenes to insure that the Badillo amendment on human rights was defeated.

It is important here to note that **originally** the "naive" Mr. Carter supported the Badillo amendment. But, Trilateral Commissioner W. Michael Blumenthal (Treasury Department) and Robert McNamara (World Bank President) straightened him out fast. From this, one receives the impression that Mr. Carter's personal beliefs are in conflict with those who dictate to him.

Colonel Edward Mandell House was renown as advisor to President Woodrow Wilson. A few years prior to his elevated status, Colonel House, during the winter of 1911, was ill at his home in Texas. There, he wrote a book entitled, **Philip Dru: Administrator.** It is a prophetical book. In it, House predicted the graduated income tax, excess profits tax, unemployment insurance, social security, and a flexible currency.[32] He also foretold of an American dictator.

"Philip Dru was a West Point graduate who resigned from the army following injury to his eyes and went into social service work. When a Wall Street conspiracy to secure absolute control over the legislative and administrative branches of the government was discovered, it led to a revolt of the people. Philip Dru assumed command of the insurgents, marched upon Washington D.C., defeated the regulars, took over the government and became dictator. During the seven years of Philip Dru's term as administrator, he revised the laws, reformed the courts, rewrote the constitution, eliminated the rich and governing class, introduced an economy of abun-

dance, and returned the government to the people. A new Monroe Doctrine was formulated, the Americas unified, and harmony established between the United States and all other nations."[33]

Is the present predicament in the nation's capitol setting the stage for the fulfillment of House's prophecy?

Senator Mathias' (Maryland) Testimony before a House Judiciary Subcommittee - 1975.

These hundreds of statutes clothe the President with virtually unlimited powers with which he can affect the lives of American citizens in a host of all-encompassing ways. This vast range of powers, taken together, confers enough authority on the President to rule the country without reference to normal constitutional processes.

Under the authority delegated by these statutes, the President may: seize property; organize and control the means of production; seize commodities; assign military forces abroad; institute marital law; seize and control all transportation and communication; regulate the operation of private enterprise; restrict travel; and, in a plethora of particular ways, control the lives of all American citizens.

Source - **Remnant Review** - 1976.[34]

Executive Order 11921 begins, "WHEREAS our national security is dependent upon our ability to assure continuity of government, at every level, in any national emergency type situation that might conceivably confront the nation; and WHEREAS effective national preparedness planning to meet such an emergency, including a massive nuclear attack, is essential to our national survival; . . . ."

(b) The departments and agencies of the Federal Government are hereby severally charged with the duty of assuring the continuity of the Federal Government in any national emergency type situation that might confront the nation. To this end, each department and agency with essential functions, whether expressly identified in this order or not, shall develop such plans and take such actions, including but not limited to those specified in this order, as may be necessary to assure that it will

be able to perform its essential functions, and continue as a viable part of the Federal Government, during any emergency that might conceivably occur. These include plans for maintaining the continuity of essential functions of the department or agency at the seat of government and elsewhere, through programs concerned with: (1) succession to office; (2) predelegation of emergency authority; (3) safekeeping of essential records; (4) emergency relocation sites supported by communications and required services; (5) emergency action steps; (6) alternate headquarters or command facilities; and (7) protection of Government resources, facilities, and personnel. The continuity of Government activities undertaken by the departments and agencies shall be in accordance with guidance provided by, and subject to evaluation by, the Director of the Federal Preparedness Agency (GSA).

Source - Remnant Review - 1976.[35]

Executive Order 11921

Part 9 — Department of Commerce

Section 901. Resume of Responsibilities. The Secretary of Commerce shall prepare national emergency plans and develop preparedness programs covering:

(1) The production and distribution of all materials, the use of all production facilities (except those owned by, controlled by, or under the jurisdiction of the Department of Defense or the Atomic Energy Commission), the control of all construction materials, and the furnishing of basic industrial services except those otherwise assigned, including:

(a) Production and distribution of and use of facilities for petroleum, solid fuels, gas, electric power, and water;

(b) Production, processing, distribution, and storage of food resources and the use of food resource facilities for such production, processing, distribution, and storage;

(c) Domestic distribution of farm equipment and fertilizer;

(d) Use of communications services and facilities, housing and lodging facilities, and health, education, and welfare facilities;

(e) Production, and related distribution, of minerals as defined in Subsection 702(5), and source materials as defined in the Atomic Energy Act of 1954, as amended; and the construction and use of facilities designated as within the responsibilities of the Secretary of the Interior;

(f) Distribution of items in the supply systems of, or con-

trolled by, the Department of Defense and the Atomic Energy Commission;

(g) Construction, use, and management of civil aviation facilities; and

(h) Construction, use and management of highways, streets, and appurtenant structures; and

(i) Domestic distribution of health resources.

Source - **Remnant Review** - 1976[36]

Executive Order 11921

Part 14

(2) Regulation. Continue or resume in an emergency (a) controlling the possession, use, transfer, import, and export of atomic materials and facilities; and (b) ordering the operation or suspension of licensed facilities, and recapturing from licensees, where necessary, special nuclear materials whether related to military support or civilian activities.

Part 17 — Federal Bank Supervisory Agencies

Section 1701. Financial Plans and Programs. The Board of Governors of the Federal Reserve System, the Comptroller of the Currency, the Federal Home Loan Bank Board, the Farm Credit Administration, and the Federal Deposit Insurance Corporation shall participate with the Federal Preparedness Agency (GSA), the Department of the Treasury, and other agencies in the formulation of emergency financial and stabilization policies. The heads of such agencies shall, as appropriate, develop emergency plans, programs, and regulations, in consonance with national emergency financial and stabilization plans and policies, to cope with potential economic effects of mobilization or an attack, including, but not limited to, the following:

(1) Money and credit. Provision and regulation of money and credit in accordance with the needs of the economy, including the acquisition, decentralization, and distribution of emergency supplies of currency; the collection of cash items and non-cash items; and the conduct of fiscal agency and foreign operations.

(2) Financial institutions. Provision for the continued or resumed operation of banking, savings and loan, and farm credit institutions, including measures for the re-creation of evidence of assets or liabilities destroyed or inaccessible.

(3) Liquidity. Provision of liquidity necessary to the continued or resumed operation of banking, savings and loan, credit

unions, and farm credit institutions, including those damaged or destroyed by enemy actions.

(4) Cash withdrawals and credit transfers. Regulation of the withdrawal of currency and the transfer of credits including deposit and share account balances.

(5) Insurance. Provision for the assumption and discharge of liability pertaining to insured deposits and insured savings accounts or withdrawable shares in banking and savings and loan institutions destroyed or made insolvent.

Source - **Remnant Review** - 1976[37]

Executive Order 11921

Part 22

(9) National industrial reserve and machine tool program. Develop plans for the custody of the industrial plants and production equipment in the national industrial reserve and assist the Department of Defense, in collaboration with the Department of Commerce, in the development of plans and procedures for the disposition, emergency reactivation, and utilization of the plans and equipment of this reserve in the custody of the Administrator.

(10) Excess and surplus real and personal property. Develop plans and emergency operating procedures for the utilization of excess and surplus real and personal property by Federal Government agencies with emergency assignments or by State and local governmental units as directed, including review of the property holdings of Federal agencies which do not possess emergency functions to determine the availability of property for emergency use, and including the disposal of real and personal property and the rehabilitation of personal property.

Part 25 — Securities and Exchange Commission

Section 2501. Functions. The Securities and Exchange Commission shall collaborate with the Secretary of the Treasury in the development of emergency financial control plans, programs, procedures, and regulations for:

(1) Stock trading. Temporary closure of security exchanges, suspension of redemption rights, and freezing of stock and bond prices, if required in the interest of maintaining economic controls.

(2) Modified trading. Development of plans designed to reestablish and maintain a stable and orderly market for securities when the situation permits under emergency conditions.

(3) Protection of securities. Provision of a national records system which will make it possible to establish current ownership of securities in the event major trading centers and depositories are destroyed.

(4) Flow of capital. The control of the formation and flow of private capital as it relates to new securities offerings or expansion of prior offerings for the purpose of establishing or reestablishing industries in relation to the Nation's needs in or following a national emergency.

Part 30 — General Provisions

Section 3001. Resource Management. In consonance with the national preparedness, security, and mobilization readiness plans, programs, and operations of the Federal Preparedness Agency (GSA), under Executive Order No. 11051 of September 27, 1962, and subject to the provisions of the preceding parts, the head of each department and agency shall:

(1) Priorities and allocations. Develop systems for the emergency application of priorities and allocations to the production, distribution, and use of resources for which he has been assigned responsibility.

(2) Requirements. Assemble, develop as appropriate, and evaluate requirements for assigned resources, taking into account estimated needs for military, atomic energy, civilian, and foreign purposes. Such evaluation shall take into consideration geographical distribution of requirements under emergency conditions.

(3) Evaluation. Assess assigned resources in order to estimate availability from all sources under an emergency situation, analyze resource availabilities in relation to estimated requirements and develop appropriate recommendations and programs, including those necessary for the maintenance of an adequate mobilization base. Provide data and assistance before and after attack for national resource analysis purposes of the Federal Preparedness Agency (GSA).

Source - **Remnant Review** - 1976[38]

The Trilateral Commission

The list that follows gives . . . the names of the more prominent and "recognizable" Trilateral Commission members who are also U.S. citizens. The list is not complete, but all the names are taken directly from the official Trilateral Commission membership list.

I. W. Abel, President, United Steelworkers of America

David M. Abshire, Chairman, Georgetown University Center for Strategic and International Studies

Graham Allison, Professor of Politics, Harvard University

John B. Anderson, House of Representatives

Ernest C. Arbuckle, Chairman, Wells Fargo Bank

J. Paul Austin, Chairman, The Coca-Cola Company

George W. Ball, Senior Partner, Lehman Brothers

Lucy Wilson Benson, Former President, League of Women Voters of the United States - Under Secretary for Security Affairs

Robert R. Bowie, Clarence Dillon Professor of International Affairs, Harvard University

John Brademas, House of Representatives

Andrew Brimmer, President, Brimmer & Co.

William Brock, United States Senate

Harold Brown, Secretary of Defense

James E. Carter, Jr., Former Governor of Georgia, President

Lawton Chiles, United States Senate

Warren Christopher, Partner, O'Melveny & Myers, Deputy Secretary of State

Alden W. Clausen, President, Bank of America

William T. Coleman, Jr., Secretary, Department of Transportation

Barber B. Conable, Jr., House of Representatives

Richard N. Cooper, Frank Altshul Professor of International Economics, Yale University, Under Secretary of Economic Affairs

John C. Culver, United States Senate

Gerald L. Curtis, East Asian Institute, Columbia University

Hedley Donovan, Editor-in-Chief, Time, Inc.

Daniel J. Evans, Governor of Washington

Donald M. Fraser, House of Representatives

Richard N. Gardner, Henry L. Moses Professor of Law and International Organization, Columbia University, Ambassador to Italy

William A. Hewitt, Chairman, Deere & Company

Richard Holbrooke, Managing Editor, Foreign Policy Magazine, Assistant Secretary for East Asian & Pacific Affairs

Thomas L. Hughes, President, Carnegie Endowment for International Peace

Robert S. Ingersoll, former Ambassador to Japan

J. K. Jamieson, Former Chairman, Exxon Corporation

Edgar F. Kaiser, Jr., President & Chief Executive Officer, Kaiser Resources Ltd.

Lane Kirkland, Secretary-Treasurer, AFL-CIO

Sol M. Linowitz, Senior Partner, Coudert Brothers, Co-Negotiator for Panama Canal Treaty

Bruce K. MacLaury, President, Federal Reserve Bank of Minneapolis

Paul W. McCracken, Edmund Ezra Day Professor of Business Administration, University of Michigan

Lee L. Morgan, President, Caterpillar Tractor Company

Kenneth D. Naden, President, National Council of Farmer Cooperatives

Henry D. Owen, Director, Foreign Policy Studies Program, The Brookings Institution

David Packard, Chairman, Hewlett-Packard Company

John H. Perkins, *President, Continental Illinois National Bank & Trust Company*

Peter G. Peterson, *Chairman, Lehman Brothers*

Edwin O. Reischauer, *University Professor, Harvard University; former U.S. Ambassador to Japan*

Elliot L. Richardson, *Rep. to U. N. Law of Sea Conference*

David Rockefeller, *Chairman, Chase Manhattan Bank*

Robert V. Roosa, *Partner, Brown Bros., Harriman & Company*

William V. Roth, Jr., *United States Senate*

Henry B. Schacht, *President, Cummins Engine Company*

William W. Scranton, *Former Governor of Pennsylvania*

Anthony Solomon, *Consultant; Deputy Secretary for Monetary Affairs*

Robert Taft, Jr.

Arthur R. Taylor, *President, Columbia Broadcasting System, Inc.*

Philip H. Trezise, *Former U. S. Assistant Secretary of State for Economic Affairs*

Cyrus R. Vance

Paul C. Warnke, *Partner, Clifford, Warnke, Glass, McIlwain & Finney*

Caspar Weinberger, *Vice-President, Bechtel Corp.*

Marine v.N. Whitman, *Distinguished Public Service Professor of Economics, University of Pittsburgh*

Carrol L. Wilson, *professor of Management, Alfred P. Sloan School of Management, MIT*

Arthur M. Wood, *Chairman, Sears, Roebuck & Company*

Leonard Woodcock, *President, United Automobile Workers*
Andrew Young, *Ambassador to the United Nations*

Source - **Profiting From Uncertainty**[39]

Chapter XV

Carter's Conflict

Mr. Carter: A Peek Over the Fence

Probabilities indicate that the U.S. Ship of State will sail into a hurricane within the next six years. The captain of the ship is "tailor made" to assume the dictatorial powers already in place (Executive Orders) for the journey through the stormy seas.

Mr. Carter's political base is the awesome cartel of corporation and banking interests, supported by the Eastern educational establishment and upper echelon of labor which brought him to power. He meets the qualifications demanded by the public that Dr. McClelland listed as necessary for a crisis and warfare leader. He is at the right place at the right time. (Any of a number of crises could result in civil unrest or war which, in turn, leads to dictatorship.) Mr. Carter's skilled use of communications in this electronic age is unsurpassed. His absence of "political debt" in the Congress, coupled with a weak Congress which is away from the job five months a year, enables him to move independently. His stubbornness, his natural preference to work alone with attention to detail, concentrates the power in the White House. Mr. Carter's entrepreneural ability, his cold, calculating and potentially ruthless modus operandi are befitting a dictator. His strict upbringing, his strong discipline, reinforced by his scientific training and military education at Annapolis and as a naval officer later, qualify him for military crisis management. The evolution to a concentration of power in the

White House is the U.S. parallel of the development of Caesarism in Rome. History therefore, is on his side. Last, but not least, Mr. Carter's Southern Baptist "God is on my side" mental attitude frees him from doubting and questioning his decisions. Professor E.E. Jennings of Michigan State University, an expert on executive behavior and a long-time "President Watcher", stated of Mr. Carter, ". . . a man on a white horse . . . He is a man in search of a mission . . . . Mr. Carter has a sense of personal history . . . . Carter is the 'maximum leader type . . . .' "[1] All he needs is a crisis that demands that decisions be made immediately from the White House.

And yet, surprising as it may seem, Mr. Carter is in conflict, in tremendous tension.

Mr. Carter's political campaign, and his subsequent election to the Presidency is, from a philosophical perspective, one of the most paradoxical occurrences in the annals of American history. Mr. Carter's strong religious faith was an acknowledged undercurrent throughout the campaign. His "humble" expression of his faith in Jesus Christ as his personal Savior - basic Christianity - is an element which has been lacking from the American political scene for some time. Historic, basic, fundamental Christianity, which Mr. Carter claims is his brand of Christianity, is almost nonexistent in America today. Yet, Americans elected such a President. (A complete discussion of the Christian perspective on government, law, education, and economics can be found in the Appendix.)

There is a more important variance. Mr. Carter is in absolute conflict with those who brought him to power. Mr. Carter believes (so he says) in a supreme God. The basic belief of The Trilateral Commission, the National Council of Churches, and the nation's political and economic leaders is not in a supreme God, but in **man,** and man's ability to solve his problems on his own. (Witness the proliferation of government programs.)

The fact that Mr. Carter's beliefs have made little difference in his administration, which is similar to recent past administrations, is evidence of conflict, instability, or blatant inconsistency. It has been previously noted, under the discussion of the Badillo human rights amendment, that Mr. Carter was persuaded by Trilateralists to change his mind and kill that amendment (conflict). Perhaps the most glaring indication of conflict came at a news conference when Mr. Carter made his now famous statement on "the unfairness of life." He responded to a question on abortion. He stated, "As you know, there are many things in life that are not fair, that wealthy people can afford and poor people can't."[2] The negative response to that answer from women, liberals, and minorities still echoes in the White House. Mr. Carter hit a secular nerve center. His statement was based upon his underlying faith in the justice of a supreme God. The implications of his statement, and the immediate rejection of same, speak clearly of the discord.

Will this contentious situation endure for four years? The conflict is, by its very nature, unstable. Therefore, Mr. Carter's administration can only be erratic as long as the present situation exists. With a man of lesser will, the variance might well last for four years. But, Mr. Carter, as earlier discussed, has the make-up of a dictator. One may wonder if there will be a power confrontation between Mr. Carter and those who brought him to power, or, if Mr. Carter remains in the Trilateralists' camp, a confrontation between the Trilateralists and the rest of the nation whose interests are being sabotaged.

The timing for an erratic administration, or another national leadership crisis, given the upcoming difficult period, could not be worse. It could be the final occurrence necessary to totally alienate the American public from its government, paving the way for anarchy war, and ultimately, Caesar.

There is a chance that Mr. Carter may not be consciously aware of his conflict. He was technically trained and educated. His tendency is to function mechanically. He is not a philosopher, by training or inclination, as are not most military men or businessmen who "work with cold hard facts." Mr. Carter is susceptible. With no well thought out philosophical base, such a man is easily influenced by any whim or idea that comes along, or is currently popular. (Such seems to be the calling card of most politicians anyway). At a time when the nation needs stable, consistent, or directional leadership, lack of same could well pave the road to disaster.

Therefore, regardless of how Mr. Carter is viewed - a man knowingly in conflict with those who brought him to power, a man unknowingly in conflict with those who brought him to power, a man who compromised himself and what he believes in, a man who really does not know what he believes - he is the captain of a Ship of State apparently about to enter a storm. One finds great difficulty in exuding confidence that the journey will be completed safely.

Carter's Risk

Such a dilemma Mr. Carter faces. If, indeed, hard times are coming, he could soften the coming blows by becoming immediately consistent with the best interests of the American people. In the near future, will the shock of political chicanery hit the American people? Will it occur in the midst of economic problems and despair, and maybe during a war? The present alienation of the American people from the federal government has been widely noted. Is a real uncomfortable crisis all that is necessary for them to turn on their expensive, domineering, bureaucratic, and irrelevant federal government? Rebelling on the one hand, they will earnestly seek a leader who will "make things right" on the other. Then, the day of Caesar will have dawned. Caesar was, and will be, popular with the people. He will champion their causes. As time has passed, more and more Americans have become disenchanted with Mr. Carter. Could an about face by him now revive his former tremendous popularity, particularly during a crisis? Mr. Carter was elected by the "common man" because he (Mr. Carter) presented himself as a "good old country boy" (common man), an outsider to the Establishment. Americans remember Mr. Carter's famous words, "I will never lie to you." Have the American people been betrayed?

Continuing his present Trilateralists' drift, a position clearly not in the best interests of, and alien to, the American people could lead to his removal from office. Will Americans "finger" Mr. Carter as the cause of all their troubles and rebel in the process? If so, then Mr. Carter stands at a crossroads in American history. His successful resolution of his present conflict could spell the difference between his position in history as one of America's greatest Presidents rather than the Judas goat.

Chapter XVI

The Inevitability of War: Hegel's Dialectic

Before the German philosopher, Goerg Wilhelm Friedrich Hegel (1770-1831), man reasoned on the basis of opposites. If one thing was true, there was an opposite which was false. If one thing was right, the opposite was wrong. There existed a belief in absolutes.[1] Hegel's dialectic changed this classical way of thinking. Hegel's dialectic gave man a whole new way of seeing facts and seeking truth.[2] "By dialectic, Hegel meant the tendency both in life and in thought for a position to spawn its own opposite, and for these two extremes to be succeeded by a compromise which partakes of some elements of both of them."[3] First there is a proposal, a proposition, a theory. This is called the thesis. Its opposite is the antithesis. The merging of the two through conflict produces the resolution, the answer, which is called the synthesis. This new synthesis then becomes a thesis, and the process continues.

"It is important to realize that the Hegelian dialectic is really a formal principle which neither discloses the goal of a process nor places any value judgment on it. The dialectic can describe a continual refinement of evil as well as a continual refinement of good."[4] The ever changing thesis, antithesis, and synthesis, which is by its very nature unstable and relative, may be good, or it may be evil. Man may build up. Man may destroy. Who is to say?

It is also most critical to this discussion on war to realize that Hegel's dialectic can only be a dialectic (a logical way of investigating the truth of something) of

CONFLICT! There is a Thesis **VERSUS** Antithesis, in order to achieve the Synthesis. The **VERSUS** is the **CONFLICT!** Thus, using Hegel's dialectic, **CONFLICT** is the only road to progress and truth. It also logically follows that to the extent the Hegelian dialectic underlies any activity, there can only be conflict rather than peace and harmony for thoughts precede action. If the thought process is one of conflict, the resultant action will be one of conflict.

Two quick examples of the Hegelian dialectic are appropriate. The bloody French Revolution was achieved by a thesis (absolute, authoritarian monarchy of the Old Regime) versus an antithesis (anarchy and libertarianism of the Revolutionary period) resolved in blood produced the synthesis. A second example of the Hegelian dialectic is the thesis (male) versus the antithesis (female) resolved in the synthesis (homosexual) (unisex).

The question is rightly asked, "Given that the Hegelian dialectic is a dialectic of conflict, why is it so important?" Answer: Today the Hegelian dialectic literally saturates the world, underlies nearly all governments, economies, and institutions. The base is laid for international conflict on a scale never before witnessed by man. The omnipresence of the Hegelian dialectic make war a dead certainty.

It is undisputed that Hegel's dialectic was employed by Karl Marx in his works (dialectical materialism). And since the works of Karl Marx are the basis of the communist movement, it is easily understood why communists' revolutions have been so bloody, both initially, and as they progressed. Also, the atrocities of Lenin, Stalin, Mao, and all the rest are logical extensions of the conflict of the Hegelian dialectic. Here's why.

The Hegelian dialectic makes conflict a necessity. War, civil or international, is a form of conflict. The Hegelian dialectic is relative. The thesis, antithesis, and synthesis are always changing. With no absolutes, and all things relative, the usual result is that "might makes right". Power decides the rules for society. With all things relative to the "power", who is to say what is an atrocity to one man is not an act of mercy to another. The "power" decides, and under such conditions, men will fight to become the "power", the "god". (An examination of the theistic implications of this discussion can be found in the Appendix).

In Western civilization, the Hegelian dialectic is also pervasive. The conflict of the dialectic is evident in the struggle for existence in Darwin's "natural selection," and the evolutionary theories of "survival of the fittest." It is most important to note that the "survival of the fittest" is exactly what happens in war. Just as significant is the fact that the **term** "survival of the fittest" was coined by Herbert Spencer.

During the time of President Cleveland, social Darwinism, based upon the Hegelian dialectic, ruled supreme. The "robber barons" were zealous disciples of Herbert Spencer, who preached this pseudoscientific, biological doctrine ("survival of the fittest"). Thus, "survival of the fittest" was originally applied to American business, **not** to the natural order. Rockefeller justified his industrial monopoly under the doctrine of "survival of the fittest". In fact, he taught it to his Sunday School class.[5] Andrew Carnegie, writing about his conversion to Spencer and Darwin stated, " 'Light came as in a flood and all was clear. Not only had I gotten rid of theology and the supernatural, but I had found the truth.' "[6] The seed of conflict in American business was sown. Business today is based upon the philosophical assumptions of these disciples of Spengler, and ultimately Hegel.

With the potential ruthlessness and relativism of the

Hegelian dialectic underlying big business today, in the scamble for profits one should expect payoffs, deals with the Russians and Chinese, kickbacks, bribes, abuse of resources, abuse of labor, monopolistic actions, collusion, conspiracy, stockholder "rip-offs," environmental disregard, sabotage, espionage, publicity gimmicks, false advertising, and production of faulty and unnecessary, but highly profitable products. The Hegelian dialectic is the philosophical "logic methodology" underlying Russian and Chinese communism **and** American big business. The applications of conflict just happen to be different.

Under Hegel's dialectic, it should be obvious that big business will do whatever is necessary to "feather its nest," including collusion with government. The synthesis of the government power **and** business/banking power has been seen in The Trilateral Commission which, as has been noted in Chapter XIV, is acting in its own "relative" self-interest, contrary to the interests of the American people. The conflict between growing government power (thesis) and growing corporation power (antithesis) was resolved in The Trilateral Commission (synthesis).

It is commonly held that the consumer is king. Business competes for his money. However, with the ruthless Hegelian dialectic underlying **big** business in the United States today, the logical end result of a few monsters at the top lays to waste the concept of consumer sovereignty and service. The big producers,

> ". . . *decide what, when and how much to produce, including the volume of construction and producer goods, activity such as new plants, office buildings. etc. In other words, volume and rate of reinvestment of profits and savings determine swings in* **consumer** *demand . . . . The producer decisions, as every one knows, are governed mainly by changes in expectations of* **profit.**"[7]

(The high financial cost of entry into the fields, plus government created monopolies, limits competition.)

". . . If **consumer desire** instead of **producer greed** was the dynamic force under capitalism, the argument based on an assumed limitless frontier of needs, discoveries and technological changes, would be entirely valid. . . ."[8] But under the concept of producer greed, such is not the case. Under the present system, growth is the god in order to achieve profits. The problem comes when the geographic frontier disappears, and it has disappeared.

"The trouble now is that, in a mature phase of in-dustrialization, the point has been reached where the productive plant of the nation has an output in excess of the subsistence necessities . . . . This, of course, is why good capitalists-practical businessmen and theorists-are ever crying out for a revival of foreign trade and foreign investment . . . .[9]

. . . . Capitalism faces a dilemma it never faced before: it cannot raise living standards without reducing profits and the incentives to new investment and enterprise; at the same time it cannot maintain the necessary market for full production and employment without raising living standards or real wages at the expense of profits.

This dilemma never existed for capitalism as long as it had a frontier, rapid growth, migration and a flourishing industrial revolution in progress . . . ."[10]

Producer greed, geometric growth, and producer sovereignty go hand in hand, and are moving presently like an ever accelerating automobile running out of road. Of course, a war could be suggested as a solution to the problem on an intermediate-term basis. In the view of some, war did solve the problem in World War II. Will another war again be recommended as the answer to capitalism's growth problem?

The primary growth addicts are the multinational corporations. But multinational sovereignty, the logical end product of the dialectical capitalistic process, is running head-on into the sovereignty of each individual national entity. The synthesis can only be achieved by violent conflict as protectionism takes hold.

". . . the real issues arise from a conflict between the international strategy of private managers and a nation's need for control over its political life . . . .

. . . . The liberal vision of the pacific and mutually beneficial international order supported by growing economic interdependence is wearing very thin. The state will not be worn away by the ebb and flow of economic transactions; if need be, it will build dikes. That reality is going to be difficult for us to deal with."[11]

The Trilateralists first achieved the synthesis of power between multinational corporations and government within a country (the United States). Now, they are quite logically attempting to achieve the synthesis on an international scale. Their goal of uniting the U.S., Japan, West Germany, and the communist nations falls right in line. A super bureaucracy is the projected end result. In such a bureaucracy, with manuals of regulations descending from above, one would normally expect the nominal bureaucrats executing the regulations to have no sense of accountability, personal involvement, or moral/emotional sense of justice. After all, they would be only a link in a chain, not much different from slaves. Enforcement would contain no elements of mercy. The **Brave New World** will have arrived.

But presently, the conflict between national protectionism and corporations promoting international free trade(?) is intensifying. The international corporations are losing the conflict. The long-term economic cycles are headed down. Ludwig von Mises saw this unavoidable crisis. He stated, "Statolatry owes much to the doctrines of Hegel."[12] He also stated, "Economic nationalism is incompatible with durable peace."[13] "The philosophy of protectionism is a philosophy of war."[14]

Is there a real threat of a super bureaucracy? Multinationals thrive on growth and stability. The cycles say the time of growth and stability is over. Will multinationals go the way of the dinosaurs? If so, then a war will only delay the inevitable. During hard times, the weight of debt and immense pension liabilities (many unfunded) can only weaken them. Lack of stability through anarchy, war, climatic changes, communications disruptions, and breakdown of distribution networks will do further damage. But, most damaging of all to the multinationals will be a lack of growth.

As economist Robert L. Heilbroner stated,

"In the long run, however, the constraints on industrial production must exert an immense pressure against the profitability of corporate activity; and the possibilities for continued multinational expansion, in a world of scarcities, bitter hostilities, and intensified desire for national self-sufficiency seem very unlikely to last more than a few decades."[15]

In 1925, Dr. Raymond Pearl of Johns Hopkins University wrote a fascinating book, **The Biology of Population**

Growth. Dr. Pearl discovered that there is a law of growth which proceeds along an "S" curve. There is a slow beginning, a rapid rise, and then a levelling out. The "S" curve applies to such things as white rats, pumpkins, yeast cells, businesses and nations.[16] Robert L. Heilbroner, in **Business Civilization in Decline,** observed,

". . . *Industrial growth, or capitalist expansion, is an exponential process-a process that proceeds like a snowball, requiring continuously increasing quantities of resources and spewing forth continuously increasing quantities of wastes, simply to maintain a constant pace of expansion. No social processes of an exponential character are capable of indefinite continuance. Sooner or later all such processes must overload their environment, consuming all its nutrients or poisoning it by the waste products associated with growth. That is why curves that originally shoot upward in near-vertical fashion sooner or later bend into* "S" **shapes,** *or actually reverse themselves and go into decline."*[17]

The natural environment could put a stop to growth immediately. As Dr. Reid Bryson, Direction of the University of Wisconsin's Institute for Environmental Research, stated, ". . . And now that we're balanced so precariously between dwindling natural resources and expanding human wants, we might be prudent to think about how easily a single bad year could throw our whole social, economic, and political system into chaos . . . ."[18] Chaos is war-internal, probably international also.

It only takes a moment's reflection to realize what the crippling or death of multinationals would do to workers in the United States. All those in occupations which are not related to the production of the necessities of life, those not blessed with incountry resources, would find things quite painful. All the attorneys, accountants, clerks, and other service personnel not engaged in actual productive occupations would suffer the most. The resulting chaos as unemployment mounts, particularly among minorities, coupled with declining profits and reduced government tax intake for welfare, social security, and other relied upon government transfer payments is horrible to contemplate. Such is the primary trend now.

Chapter XVII

Conclusion

Panics are the result of surprise. Will the acceleration of the forces (cycles) bringing radical changes engulf the masses? Just as the masses in a market expect much higher prices at the top, so could the masses be absolutely shocked if their lingering expectations of good times in the future are shattered. Would a mass surprise result in violence, internal as well as international? Can the public be warned of the potential danger? For the reasons discussed in the Introduction, the masses are not inclined to listen. Historically, people resist change at all cost. Unlike members of the animal kingdom who instinctively flee danger, man sits around, clinging to illusions of security. Institutions can only change slowly. Will that be satisfactory in the near future? History says no. To think otherwise is to ignore the unending cycles of civilizations and wars. The flow of the tide eventually sweeps everything in its path. The evidence gives an ominous warning.

It may well be that during the next six years true wealth will be measured by having plenty of food to eat, water to drink, good health, and safe and warm living quarters in the midst of friends and family. The cycles say the judge with the sword is on the way. The worldwide presence of the Hegelian dialectic multiplies the scope and intensity of conflict. One can best prepare for a difficult period by doing whatever one can to become self-sufficient. Creative brainstorming with like-minded friends and family is recommended. In hard times, no man is an island. Group efforts and support are a must.

Start with the basics. Self-sufficiency in the production of food, water, shelter, clothing, and energy are the categories deserving attention. A garden, greenhouse, hydroponics system, plus the raising of small animals such as rabbits, milk goats, and chickens, are excellent in the food production area. Property on a creek or near a body of water, a spring, a windmill, a cistern - all fulfill the water self-sufficiency requirements. A well-insulated dwelling with a wind or solar energy source makes sense, as does a wood heat and cook stove. Underground protection is a must. An oversupply of clothing for all seasons is recommended. Provision for self-defense goes without saying. Excess capital should be applied toward barter items and real money - gold and silver coins.

As is said in real estate, the three most important considerations are location, location, and location. At a certain point of time in the near future, living in the cities could be the equivalent of holding a stick of lighted dynamite. The best locations would then be in rural communities that meet the following criteria:

1. Low crime rate, traditional American values of hard work and self-sufficiency, conservative political leanings, ethics based on absolutes
2. Racial harmony
3. A widely dispersed local population (low population density)
4. Necessary skills widely distributed in the local population (medical, dental, carpentry, etc.)
5. No potential military targets within a 100-mile radius
6. No large government installations of any type
7. Favorable wind currents and climate that provide ample moisture, favorable growing conditions, and no danger of fallout

8. More than a tank of gas removed from any major city
9. A commodity-based economy
10. Low risk of earthquake, volcanic activity, flood, and fire.

There is no such thing as neutralizing all risks. There is no place on earth where all of the above criteria are perfectly met. Life itself is a risk. Perfect security does not exist. Lack of perfection, however, does not justify a "let's eat, drink and be merry" attitude. Risk must be managed. That is the prudent man's approach. This work has attempted to show, that during the next six years, the risk of war is very high. In light of this, priority should be given to preparation for the coming difficult times.

The REAPER

Your Life Line to the Future

The author who brought you *CYCLES OF WAR* edits *The Reaper*, a weekly trading advisory service that is the natural extension of *Cycles of War*, plus more! *The Reaper* focuses on the timing for personal and financial actions within the framework of the national and international political, economic, and financial arenas. Its unique insight keeps its readers far ahead of the thundering masses, a must for survival today. Just one idea could save you, or make you, many, many times its subscription price. At this dangerous time in the world's history, you must be a member of the aware elite. Join *The Reaper's* informed family now!

The Reaper
P.O. Box 27554
Phoenix, Arizona 85061

The greatest bargain available to man is the low cost of good advice. Your very first issue of *The Reaper* will verify this.

Gentlemen:
  Begin my subscription to *The Reaper* immediately.

☐ 1 year — $195
☐ 6 mo. — $110
☐ 5 issue trial — $25
    Check or money order enclosed.

☐ Information only

Name: ....

Address: ....

City: .... State: .... Zip: ......

Phone: ....

Appendix

At a time in the world's history when problems are overwhelming, it makes sense to explore fresh, maybe even radical approaches in an attempt to solve the difficulties. This writer, as a result of research into the implications of Mr. Carter's Christianity as would be applied by his administration, had his eyes opened. Indeed, it appears that each man plants a seed of faith. He either places his faith in God, or in man. It seems to be an either/or matter. The first option is a decision based in humility; the second is based in pride. From each of these individual decisions which, in turn, make up the collective "mass mind" spring all the institutions - government, legal, educational, and economic, just to mention four.

What follows is heavy reading. The quotes are lengthy and extensive. But rather than restate or paraphrase, this writer felt it was critical to provide complete exposure for insightful, little known authors who have a powerful understanding and a creative solution to today's dismal state of affairs.

The Importance of Ideas

The man on the street is unconsciously influenced by the thinking of philosophers. A philosophical idea drifts down from the philosopher, to the intellectuals and educators, and then to the workers, and finally to the upper middle class.[1] The average American today has within him a parentally and culturally indoctrinated value structure and frame of reference which serves as the basis of his thinking and decisions. Since the formation of this (also known as norms and standards) is seldom a conscious process, it is not surprising to find the society at large expressing the basic faith (presupposition) of the public school system as well - humanism, the sovereignty of man. The sum total of all this mass thinking makes up the nation which, in turn, elects the government. Good results are the product of correct thinking. Confusion, chaos, and war are the results of poor thinking. A change in thinking requires a change in the value structure, a change in basic beliefs (presuppositions), which are located at the bottom of the thought process. It is important to remember that what is being dealt with here are assumptions upon which men operate. They are unprovable. "The answers to the great questions of life cannot be discovered by finite human minds, are unsolvable by human reason, lie lost in the mists of the unknown, and that, consequently, we do not know and never will know . . . ."[2] The exception to this, of course, is the Hebrew/Christian concept of special revelation where the transcendent makes itself known to the finite.[3]

Mr. Carter claims that he subscribes to this concept of special revelation. By so doing, he has placed himself in a position of logical inconsistency with his governmental programs. This inconsistency is by its very nature unstable. Most would consider this to be an unacceptable position for a President burdened with the responsibilities of the highest office of the world.

Presupposition - Assumed Fact or Truth, Basic Faith or Belief

God	versus	Man
Humility	versus	Pride

By basic Christianity is meant that Mr. Carter believes in a personal, infinite, triune God who controls history, who is sovereign, and who additionally enjoys the attributes of absolute justice and righteousness, love, eternal life, omniscience, omnipresence, omnipotence, immutability, and veracity. Mr. Carter believes in the doctrines of the hypostatic union of Christ, the virgin birth, plenary inspiration, the total depravity of man with personal salvation coming through the humble act of acceptance of Jesus Christ as personal Savior.[4] Mr. Carter has continually reaffirmed that the most important thing in his life is his relationship with "The Lord". He has apparently faced the historical evidence and issue of the Cross and made the decision that Jesus Christ is divine. He has rejected the only other three logical interpretations, that is, Jesus was a charlatan, a lunatic, or his disciples were charlatans, lunatics, or naive exaggerators.[5] His status quo is one of humility; he saw his need, as a sinner, for a personal Savior. His faith is God-centered, not self-centered, with all knowledge, truth, and wisdom emanating from Above. Man is the clay, and God is the Potter. Mr. Carter is a servant to God's will for his life. The eminent theologian, Cornelius Van Til put it this way, " 'Either presuppose God and live, or presuppose yourself as ultimate and die. That is the alternative with which the Christian must challenge his fellow man.' "[6]

By contrast, the world's system is humanism. "Humanism . . . is the system whereby man, beginning absolutely by himself, tries to build out from himself having only man as his integration point to find all knowledge meaning and value."[7] Humanism is the sovereignty of man. The position that man, by man's efforts, can solve man's problems is one of pride. Basic Christianity condemns pride as the worst of sins, ". . . an abomination unto the Lord."[8]

152

Logic Methodology - Way of Thinking

Antithesis (Opposites)	**versus**	Hegel's dialectic (Thesis vs. antithesis results in synthesis)
Cause and effect, linear, with absolutes		Relativism

The Christian concept of faith, in the sense of "logic methodology," is a belief in opposites and absolutes. It is a common misconception that the contrasting Hegelian dialectic can be achieved by pure reason. Although Hegel thought this was possible, that synthesis could be achieved by reason, the "father of modern thinking," Soren Kierkegaard, concluded that synthesis could only be achieved by a "leap by faith." So, no matter how one cuts it, faith in opposites (the antithesis) (God), or faith in the Hegelian dialectic (man as god), man is forced to make a "leap of faith."

The concept of opposites, absolutes - the antithesis - is the base upon which historic Christianity stands. Therefore, any system of logic, any way of thinking that is not based upon the antithesis, is in conflict with basic Christianity. Cause and effect is also Christian in that it is related to the antithesis.

By contrast, under the relative and unstable Hegelian dialectic, there are only pragmatic considerations, no absolutes. Man necessarily then becomes the absolute because all things are relative to man and his wishes. In other words, man becomes his own god. But man as god is problematic.

Man is not sovereign in the natural universe. Thus, under dialectical humanism, man is in irreconcilable conflict with the real world that he experiences every day. As such, he is also irrational.

"All systems of thought which rest on the humanistic assumption that the mind of man is

capable of achieving all truth and that man is sovereign, possessing the inherent and inalienable right to decide the truth, or even deciding if truth exists, must bear the stigma of irrationalism." [9]

("The Biblical concept of justification is a total personal antithesis."[10])

Education

| Unified field of knowledge | **versus** | Divided field of specialized knowledge |

Today the State controls the educational process - mandatory State education through almost the first two decades of life. And since the education is "free", the large majority of Americans are educated in the public school system. Thus, the assumed truth of the public school system permeates society, government, religion, economics - all aspects of American life. Frederic N. Andre and Rousas John Rushdoony in an article entitled, "The Adversary Concept," which appeared in **The Journal of Christian Reconstruction,** declared;

"State schools, (so-called public education) are relativistic to the core, and John Dewey and others very early declared the enemy or adversary to be supernatural Christianity. Of the ideas of the saved and the lost, heaven and hell, good and evil, Dewey said that it represented a 'spiritual aristocracy' and an alien creed. 'I cannot understand how any realization of the democratic ideal as a vital moral and spiritual ideal in human affairs is possible without a surrender of the conception of the basic division to which supernatural Christianity is committed.' " [11]

John Dewey is considered to be the father of modern American education. Education today is seen as the means by which man will solve man's problems. It is thus man oriented, humanistic, relativistic (All in the family).

William N. Blake wrote "Van Til's Vision for Education" in a volume entitled **Foundations of Christian Scholarship.** There he stated,

"Pedagogy and consequently the teaching profession has been under steady attack since John Dewey's philosophy seized the attention and loyalty of the teaching profession. The dismal morass into which this kind of thinking has led the profession offers no hope for the restoration of learning and of the consequent respect for teacher . . . ." [12]

It comes as no surprise that, as **U.S. News & World Report** stated,

"Summer's sunset is bringing growing worries about the state of education. Plunging test scores, dwindling enrollments, climbing costs — these factors put taxpayers in poor mood to shell out for local schools. Polls show skepticism about how well schools prepare students for work." [13]

Today's schools, particularly in the cities, are battlegrounds, where achievement of discipline is considered to be a major success.[14] The July 18, 1977 issue of **U.S. News & World Report** featured an article entitled, "America's Youth: Angry . . . Bored . . . or Just Confused?" "Another generation of troubled youth is on stage across America, with new discontents and hangups . . . ."[15] America's youth are in extreme tension. The educational system help put them there. They are taught fragmented bits of information. There is no unity of thought. Knowledge does not integrate. It simply does not fit all together. **U.S. News** notes, "At an all-time high are teenage suicides, violent crime, vandalism, pregnancies, drug abuse and alcoholism."[16] Why not? Everything taught is relative. There is no stability, no right or wrong. Eat drink, and be merry, and then, for a release of tension, rip up the world and oneself in the process. Self-destruction is the inevitable end result. The educational concept of God as the unifying entity of knowledge is foreign to students today. Blake continues,

"The theory of evolution largely governs educational methodology today. According to this view the mind and personality of the child are determined by his environment because man originally developed through successive environmental changes and undergoes similar growth now. Man's creator is thus nature, not God. Man is accordingly passive toward his creator, i.e., his environment. Part of this environment is his community and state. Is it any wonder that increasing numbers of people view themselves in a passive role over against the government, hereby overthrowing the Christian position that government is the responsibility of people? On the other hand, a minority of activist students - often very bright - want to take control of the reins of power in order to reshape their environment, thereby reshaping mankind. They become technological experts, managers of society, planners; or they become revolutionaries who in some way are motivated by Marx's words: 'The philosophers have only interpreted the world, in various ways; the point, however, is to change it.' In either case, the result of such unbridled humanism - men

playing God - is the end of human freedom. Academically, the result tends to be the production of dull, academic drones or lawless student revolutionaries. Here, too, the alternatives spell the death of education. Van Til shows the dangers of not making 'the Creator-creature distinction absolutely fundamental' in one's thinking. Christian educators have the foundation for a methodology that will produce stalwart men. In the Christian methodology, the human being is seen as master of his environment, precisely because he is under the sovereignty of a Creator God. Any psychology of methodology in education that fails to establish itself squarely on the doctrine of creation strips man of his dignity and is accordingly illiberal." [17]

How ironic that humanism, the sovereignty of man, results in the illiteracy and slavery of man.

There is no conflict here with what Blake is stating and the concept of cycles. Blake obviously recognizes that man is master of his environment within certain limits. In other words, man is not master of his environment in the sense that he can dictate when the sun will rise, or when it will set, or when the seasons will change. These cycles do not involve action by man, nor do they come under the influence of man. Man can, however, make decisions within the framework of these cycles. His volition functions within the boundaries of the natural order.

Cycles, such as warfare cycles, on the other hand, involve decisions by man, and thus man can influence such cycles. That is why cycles involved with human action are probabilistic. They can expand, contract, or disappear. Thus, there are cyclical conditions which have a tendency to push man to war. (A colder, drier, climate is one condition discussed in Chapter Four.) Knowledge of the cycle is a helpful defense against its occurrence. What is likely, however, is that under the doctrine of humanism, man is unstable and much more likely to drift under the influence of the cyclical conditions and, in this case, go to war, because he lacks the anchor of God. The humility of man, recognizing his subservience to God, and God's natural laws (including cycles) is the key to his enlightment, growth, and edification. True learning comes by listening, not thinking one's own thoughts. Learning is thus based in humility. The Christian perspective is that ". . . man must think God's thoughts after Him if he is to know anything. How does one know whether he is thinking God's thoughts? To the extent that God's thoughts are revealed to us in Scripture, to this extent can we think His thoughts after Him."[18]

Education in the historical Christian sense holds that learning and work are an integrated whole, and that there is a unity over the whole field of knowledge since God is the Creator and all things relate to Him under his Creation. As such, in the world today, there are few truly educated men. "True education means thinking by association across the various disciplines. . . ."[19] One example would be the ability to see how the laws of thermodynamics apply to money, for money is nothing more than a form of energy. Since energy can be neither created nor destroyed, only transferred, it logically follows that money as a form of energy can be neither created nor destroyed, only transferred. Thus, government cannot create wealth; it can only redistribute it.

By contrast, the State educational system yields a divided field of knowledge. Today one finds a world of narrow specialists with parts but no whole. Logically then, under the Christian concept, these educated specialists should have great difficulty relating to the real world, and further, since the "educated" are at the head of government as well as schools, severe problems should be expected in the society at large.

Irving Kristol, resident scholar at the American Enterprise Institute hinted at this problem in an article in the **Wall Street Journal** entitled, "On the Unfairness of Life." Speaking of the era when the Christian concept of absolutes and God was dominant, he stated,

> "Well, that was in another world, and in another age - an 'age of faith,' as our textbooks so condescendingly put it. We sophisticated moderns, more educated and more advanced than our forebears, are not about to tolerate any such metaphysical consolations. We demand results, here and now. We insist that reality exists to be rectified, not to be accepted and certainly never to be celebrated. Our faith is in the combined power of indignation, reason and compassion to rid the world of all its evils . . . . **Time** magazine . . . solemnly informs us that 'the ultimate morality or immorality . . . need not be decided in order to judge the principle of unfairness.' In short, 'fairness' has nothing to do with morality, but only with equality. Wrongness equally shared is 'fairer' than rightness unequally shared. [Who makes the decision? This is relativism.] If anyone had any doubt as to the strength - the mindless strength - of the egalitarian temper in our times, this little episode should surely dispel it.
>
> . . . . Interestingly enough, the more educated you are, the more likely you are to be victimized by such passions. There seems to be something about our educational system, and the culture, which ultimately governs its

operations, which permanently transports its population out of the world of common sense. Perhaps I should emphasize that word 'permanently', since it is always a part of education, properly understood, to elevate the student temporarily beyond the common sense world. But it is absurd and irresponsible to leave him there, since that world-of fantasy, of speculation, of pure reason - is not the world he is going to have to live in. Coming back to earth is also part of the educational enterprise." [20]

Kristol continued,

"It is the lack of 'higher education' of this sort that explains why ordinary men and women tend to be more sensible about life's real or supposed 'unfairness'. They think you are lucky if you are born handsome, healthy and clever, and they do not think nature is wickedly 'unfair' in not making everyone equally gifted. And since they do not subscribe to the Rousseauian doctrines that man is innately good and only society corrupts, or that all inequalities are superfluous excrescences on the social order, they do not accept all claims of 'unfairness' at face value." [21]

Kristol has confirmed that the world of the uneducated, the real world, is far removed from the world of the educated. The remarks he makes about the perspective of the world held by the educated is consistent with the "unreality" of humanism.

Humanism focuses on the equality of man, and this doctrine is promulgated through the schools. Kristol cites a European experience,

". . . a commission of the European Community took a public opinion poll on the subject of poverty. It discovered that, in all the nations of

Western Europe, people who are well-educated and well-off tended to blame poverty on 'social injustice.' On the other hand, the less well-educated and less well-off tended to think that, if people were poor, it was at least partly their own doing." [22]

Kristol concludes, ". . . politics . . . can never reconstruct the human condition, of which 'unfairness' is a recalcitrant feature. For that reconstruction-more properly called redemption-someone other than the politician or the bureaucrat will be needed."[23] How about a God?

Just prior to World War II, Lawrence Dennis, anticipating the United States' involvement in the war, wrote a farsighted book entitled, **The Dynamics of War and Revolution.** With regard to education he stated,

". . . The role of education in our present crisis is to make the masses susceptible as they never were before to propaganda and demagogic manipulation. The greater the number of people who can vote and read, the greater the irrationality, the greater the conflict of minority interests and the greater the anarchy in the political and economic processes under a system of parliamentary democracy. The people can rule with rationality and success only through a single ruler, party and governing agency . . . .

Democracy and education have not brought peace or social justice. On the contrary, they have intensified and implemented class warfare with new techniques . . . ." [24]

So, not only does humanistic education today lead

to a godlessness that is in conflict with the natural order, but it also paves the way for social clashes and then Caesar.

Political System

| Limited government | **versus** | Pervasive government (Socialism, Communism) |
| Law based on Judeo/ Christian absolutes | **versus** | Law is relative |

The political system, Biblically espoused, is one of limited government. Since God is sovereign and perfect justice, His law is Supreme. Thus, human governments fulfill only limited functions such as providing for the national defense, administering justice when disputes arise between individuals, and settling questions of God's law. This was clearly the governmental function of the Judges in the Old Testament in Samuel I & II.[25] Judges 21:25 states, "In those days there was no king in Israel; every man did what was right in his own eyes." As Frederick Nymeyer states in **Minimal Religion,**

"The Hebrew-Christian ethic leaves everything free between men, except (1) no coercion, (2) no theft, (3) no fraud, (4) no adultery, (5) no envy; and (6), it requires respect to parents.

The rest of life is left both unprohibited or uncommanded. Do what you will; live your own life your own way; eat, drink and be merry, if you will; or work, slave and save; be pleasant or be a curmudgeon; have your own goals; do not let your parents dominate your adult life; pick your own wife (or husband), and leave your parents." [26]

(It should be noted **Minimal Religion** interprets

Scripture in a strict sense. Also, the Christian laws for society at large, which are minimal in nature, do not represent all the doctrines which govern life for the "born again" Christian believer in the family of God. Once in the Christian family, a whole series of doctrines, intended for the edification of the believer, come into play.)

> *"Freedom was too great an area to be defined in the Decalogue. It was better to specify the few things forbidden . . . . The* **negative** *feature of these ethical rules constitutes one of its admirable features. Good laws generally are negative.*

> *. . . . . a man whose* **method** *of helping himself is by injuring his neighbor will find the law burdensome, and may land in jail. But the man whose method is to operate by voluntary contracts with his neighbor (without using forbidden methods) will prosper, will be popular, will be 'free'.*

> *. . . . . But the law which the Hebrew-Christian religion prescribes is limited to prohibiting injury to others. It is a minimum of law.*

> *The application of its ethical rule is not made to depend, in the Hebrew-Christian system, on some form of government. . . .*

> *. . . the rule applies to* **any** *organization of society — a monarchy, an aristocracy, a republic, or a democracy."* [27]

Christian ethics are individualistic not egalitarian. Government's purpose is to ". . . defend, to protect, to prevent violence, fraud, and other predatory acts.

Other endeavors are to be left to the initiative and choices of people acting voluntarily, either jointly or as individuals . . ." [28]

Mr. Carter's government is a far cry from the principles of basic Christianity which he affirms. One might also notice that "big government" is desired and supported today by organized religion. Therefore, organized religion in the United States today is in opposition to basic Christianity. Well! Actually, that should come as no surprise. It was organized religion, the Pharisees and Sadducees, who put Christ on the Cross.

And since this is a book on warfare, and presently the discussion is contrasting organized religion and "big government" with basic Christianity, it needs to be said that it is organized religion, in the name of humanity, that supports wars.

The nations of the world have no common culture, set of values, norms and standards, or even the same interests. That is a fact. Basic Christianity says fine. A nation can do what it will as long as it does not cause injury to others. It is the self-righteousness of organized religion that calls the troops to arms, not over the reality of conflicting self-interest (in most cases), but over rules, by invoking law and morality - principles. It is the appeal to ethics that ignites the fuse of war, and there are no common ethics internationally. [29]

Ideology has caused the United States trouble historically with Mexico, Haiti, Nicaragua, and got the country involved in World War I and II, or was at least the rallying cry. It is presently the basis of U.S. involvement in South Africa. It seems the piousness of government and organized religion refuses to stoop to the reality of arguments over things. They prefer the elevated status of debate over words, usually in the form of international law.[30] To be the self-appointed policeman of the world is intrusive, self-righteous, and contrary to basic Christianity. Mr. Carter comes to mind as a man whose high sense of principle is a natural catalyst for war. It is a manifestation of pride for a country or its President to believe it/he knows what is best for another country or person.

Today primarily Conservatives and Libertarians argue for the Christian perspective of government, but they do not do so under the banner of Christianity. Lawrence D. Pratt, in "The Politics of Pragmatism: Threat to Freedom", stated,

> *"Conservatives, even those who profess to be Christians, all too often have accepted the secularist argument that their religious doctrines do not apply to worldly affairs . . . .*
>
> *Even pagans have recognized that conclusions are the result of their premises; . . . .*
>
> *No matter how close to the surface of an argument may be the actual major premise of a contemporary American politician or academician, pragmatism is the rationale most often offered . . . .*
>
> *Instead of clearly setting forth the major premise . . . vague words capable of being construed in a wide variety of ways are employed . . . . 'Needs' and 'social justice' are examples of frequently employed charismatic terms capable of providing an emotionally laden moralistic cover for any number of schemes designed to curry favor for a proposition.*
>
> *Orwell, in observing the rhetoric used to justify the operation of the totalitarian regimes of*

the twentieth century, observed that abstract words employed as charismatic terms become so free from any concrete references, that nobody blinks when these regimes claim that 'Slavery is Freedom.'

The nineteenth-century classical liberal view of freedom, confident in its faith in man's autonomous rationality and will, argued that freedom should be understood in terms of the absence of coercion and fraud. As modern autonomous man began to realize his estrangement from other men and the universe about him, freedom came to be understood in terms of the power needed to control a lawless universe. Without power to protect himself in a universe of chance, men increasingly felt desperate and meaningless.

The evolution of the classical liberal's laissez-faire doctrine into the contemporary liberal's programs for statist compulsion that have increasingly claimed sovereignty over all aspects of an individual's life is but a record of the dialectical tension inherent in the presuppositions of the claims of autonomous man . .

. . . . The consequences of men claiming to organize governments independent of God's law have followed the same pattern of oscillation between individualism and statism as has occurred in the case of liberalism over the course of a century. To assume that man's mind is as ultimate as God's, and therefore to conceive of the universe as a world of chance, requires one to posit the locus of sovereignty apart from God somewhere else in a universe that is greater than both man and God. As it *happens, men have posited two basic possibilities for the source of sovereignty apart from God: the individual or the state.*

The cause of the defense of freedom has suffered because conservatives have been unwilling to face the true nature of the threat of tyranny. The attempts to formulate a system of nontyrannical government most often employed by conservatives have been either the warm cocoon of an organic tradition or the brave adventurousness of the rugged individualist. In either case, sovereignty has not been recognized to be God's alone. As a result, the conservative has based his defense of freedom on the same presuppositions as those used by tyrants and outlaws to justify their actions.

The most systematic is the libertarian conservative's positing of sovereignty in the individual, the more clearly does his view of man resemble Rousseau's or that portrayed in Marx's post-withering-of-the-state utopia. This is necessarily so because the thoroughgoing libertarian has presupposed that all values are relative and only apply to each individual. To assume that all that is required for harmony in the relations among normless men is the removal of force where its monopoly has been ordained by God is to assume that man is so well-intentioned that he needs no general law.

The more systematic is the traditionalist conservative's positing of sovereignty in existing institutions and the organic, unruptured development of institutions, the more clearly does he share the pharaonic view that there are only two classes of men-the rulers and the ruled: or the similar Bolshevik view of the enlightened vanguard in whose hands History has placed the fate of the rest of mankind. Justifying institutions because they function stably (the Soviet Union, for one) hardly provides the basis for condemning an established tyranny. Much of the history of mankind is the long history of stable despotisms . . . .

. . . Are institutions as institutions to be the cornerstone of life? Or perhaps, stable institutions? But again, why institutions, why stability? Why not war and circuses?

It has only been the systematic theist, i.e., Biblical Christians, who have clearly set forth the basis of society in terms of a straightforward exposition of their presuppositions. The dialectical shiftings of the 'neutral' reason of autonomous man can provide no protection against the demagogic promises of the statist. This is so even when attempts are made to rise above pragmatism since man's ultimate concerns are not made dependent on God. Only the revealed law of the Bible can protect man's freedom from the usurpations of the state that claims total allegiance as the sovereign source of all law in exchange for its putative protection of alienated men afloat in a sea of randomness . . . .

. . . . That the hedonistic attitudes fostered by socialism ramify in a country's foreign policies was observed in Britain by C. Northcoate Parkinson in his book, **Left Luggage.** *As the something-for-nothing lusts of the citizenry are whetted by statist programs, public opinion in a democratic country increasingly militates against defense expenditures of even the most obvious sort . . . .*

. . . The pragmatist may often be heard to argue against the obvious excesses of the openly diabolical, but the pragmatist himself has accepted the same presuppositions as has the open champion of tyranny. 'As a man speaks, so he is.'

It is unfortunately only a matter of time before the pragmatist is forced to yield his temperamental defenses against the excesses of tyranny in the face of the logic of tyranny. Neither the pragmatist nor the statist advocate of tyranny accepts the sovereignty of God as the foundation for all government, so neither the pragmatist nor the statist can put forth a viable defense of freedom." [31]

Of the substitution of the State for the Biblical God, Kristol declared, "The locus . . . of power is government, and it is plausible to think that the rise of powerful, centralized governments in our century has a significant connection with the decline of religion."[32] Douglas Hyde, many years Secretary of the Communist Party in Great Britain, stated that,

"Communism was, for him, a substitute religion . . . . 'Communism . . . has its origins in precisely that spiritual vacuum which exists all over what once was Christendom . . . . One has to be potentially good or intelligent,' he insists, 'even to be aware that it is not enough simply to drift along without sense of purpose or direction, with neither faith nor ideal. That is why Communism so often claims the best-those who feel the miss. It is why it has spread in our day and no other. I would say,' he accuses, 'that the majority who come to Communism do so because, in the first instance, they are sub-

consciously looking for a cause which will fill the void left by unbelief.' " [33]

The godlike status of the State can also be seen in the historical rise and subsequent deification of the Caesars.

The majority of the world today falls under the type of pervasive government known as communism or socialism. The works of the atheistic philosopher, Karl Marx, are the foundation of these systems. Marx's logic methodology was Hegel's dialectic. This relativism and resultant humanism has resulted in fewer "human rights." As Peter Berger stated in **The Wall Street Journal,** in "The Link Between Capitalism and Democracy,

"Put differently again, there is not a single Socialist country with a democratic form of government. And it is difficult to find a Socialist country with a passable record on human rights, including the so-called economic rights of which the left is so enamored." [34]

Clarence B. Carson observed,

"The engine of Marxism is hatred, hatred for everything as it is, hatred of religion, hatred of the family, hatred of the division of labor, hatred of the state, hatred of capitalists, hatred of property, hatred of the 'rural idiocy' of farmers, and yes, hatred of industrial workers . . . .

The modus operandi of Marxism is destruction. That is the true meaning of Marxian revolution . . . . All the actuality that has been accumulated through the ages must be destroyed-property relationships, religious belief, family ties, legal forms, the intellectual heritage, culture, and civilization itself. How else, but by tyranny, can such a destruction be wrought?

Tyranny is embedded in the very framework of Marxism . . . .

. . . . The appeal of Marxism lies in the fact that it justifies and sanctifies the release of the demonic urges in each of us. It justifies and sanctifies hate, envy, the love of power, the bent to destruction, the desire to set everything right (particularly others), and all the vague and unfulfilled longings of men . . . ."[35]

The way of Marxism is far removed from the Christian concept of government's limited place in the scheme of things. Carson's comments also reveal the full, evil, destructive fury of the atheistic, Marxist application of the dialectic.

Rousas John Rushdoony, commenting on today's political situation stated, "The locale of unity, in Hegelianism, is the State."[36] But he later declared that the logic of the sovereignty of man has come to mean the sovereignty of man in the mass.[37] But the sovereignty of man, the logic of humanism, eventually necessitates that every man be his own god and that no one be coerced. Thus, the State is only a substitute god. This resultant anarchy was clearly recognized by Max Stirner, the great thinker of anarchism. Karl Marx viciously attacked Stirner because Marx recognized that,

"Anarchism . . . meant the collapse of humanism into disorder and defeat. The way out was socialism, the sovereignty of the scientific socialist order and its freedom to remake man into that 'free' condition where he would naturally function in terms of an over-riding humanistic plan.

Thus, in one form or another, the sovereign-

ty of man has led to the enslavement of man, breakdown of social order . . . .

Apart from the sovereignty of God, society has no real principle of law and order. The logic of Stirner is the logic of humanism, of the sovereignty of man. Stirner argued that all men who have any moral hesitation about incest are still Christians, because they are governed by something other than their will. Truly sovereign man knows no law except his own will and desire. Because the truly sovereign man can tolerate no other sovereign, it is moral necessity for him to defy every law of God and man. As Sartre recognized, freedom then becomes negation. The result, whether in politics or art, is a program of rebellion, revolution, and negation.

This then is the necessary course of the modern world, rebellion, revolution, and negation, as long as it remains faithful to its humanistic faith.

The alternative, the sovereignty of God, declares that there is a mandatory law and order . . . ." [38]

"As Dostoyevsky saw, if there is no God, then everything is permitted.

. . . . Nietzsche and others, the Marquis de Sade included, all argued that, because there is no God, there is no law.

. . . . When all values are reduced to nothing, then only power establishes value, and death is the means whereby this new value is applied." [39]

We have witnessed the all powerful State. It is

breaking up into the logical result of humanism - anarchy. Anarchy is followed by power which can inflict death, power historically held by a Napoleon or a Caesar.

Law

Any system of morality is an expression of religion, for it is concerned with ideas about ultimacy and values. "Law is enacted morality."[40] The procedures for the enactments of law are procedures for the enactment of morality. Law is established and enforced by the State. Therefore, the logical sequence is as follows: religion, morality, law, State - all part of the same family. Therefore, "Every law structure or system is an establishment of religion. There can be no separation of religion and the State."[41] This is a most critical point, and has not crossed the minds of most Americans. The separation of church and state is an impossibility in intellectual practice. Church and State can only be separated institutionally.

"Moreover, the modern idea of law, both in the church and in open humanistic circles, is radically flawed and rests essentially on a Hegelian and Darwinian world view . . . ." [42]

. . . . In any system of thought, the source of law is the sovereign. If the sovereign is man, then existential man is his own law. If the sovereign is the State, or the dictatorship of the proletariat, then that agency is the source of law. Law is inseparable from sovereignty, and the god of any system can be quickly identified by locating the source of law . . . .

It is of critical importance that biblical law be restored to its rightful place of authority because humanism is in radical decay, as is its law.

Humanistic law has as its logical sovereign every man as his own god, and therefore his own law. The result is anarchy . . . .[43]

. . . . The false note in Orwell's **1984** *and in* **Future Corruption** *is the assumption that, with man's radical perversity, totalitarian regimes will still be the order of the day in the future. They presuppose the disappearance of all Christian virtues save one: obedience. In the Soviet Union, precisely because total terror is irrational and strikes at guilty and innocent alike, there is an increasing resistance to the required order. If an innocent man is so readily tossed into a slave labor camp to provide slave labor, as Solzhenitsyn's* **Gulag Archipelago** *has shown, who bother to be innocent or obedient?*

The pattern in every part of the world, as humanism spreads its cancer, is of a growing lawlessness . . . ."[44]

But anarchy and lawlessness cannot last long. Nymeyer succintly states why.

". . . anarchy . . . is not a viable — survivable — system for two reasons: (1) men are generally not good enough to be permitted to be anarchists; and (2) ambitious evil men do not fail to attempt to fill the vacuum created by 'no law,' and they usually succeed; they seize power. The customary course then is from anarchy to tyranny; . . . ."[45]

Anarchy unlocks Caesar's door.

The relative and distorted concept of present day law, with its humanistic and "social justice" applications of "equality" has been noted by respected contemporary writers. Kirstol commented,

"Since inequality equals 'unfairness', and since society and all its institutions create and tolerate inequalities, the proper and humane attitude toward social reality is one of indignant anger, now identified with 'idealism.' What is 'unfair' ought not to be; someone or something is to blame; and a good government will not permit such inequity/inequality. And so it is that, out of an inflamed sense of compassion and a utopian insistence on 'social justice' in the here and now, modern politics-what we still call 'liberal' politics-mobilizes the passions that will eventually destroy it." [46]

Ralf Dahrendorf in a **Wall Street Journal** article entitled, "Is Britain Really That Sick?", quoted Samuel Brittan.

"Equality 'has now turned sour, and it has done immense damage to my country,' says Samuel Brittan, pointing out that there is no 'invisible hand' in the political market: 'There is nothing to prevent the rivalry of coercive groups from reaching a stage where nonnegotiable claims add up to more than the total national product.' " [47]

Kristol and Brittan are documenting the State's manifestation of "equality" humanism in its terminal stage.

The unstable relativism of humanism is the real enemy to both Christianity and stable protection under law.

". . . For relativism, there is no good and evil, only pragmatic considerations. Its absolute is thus man, not God. All things are relative to man and man's wishes, because man is the absolute or God of modern thought, or humanism. God is thus the great enemy, and law, order, morality,

and everything that smacks of God is to warred against.

. . . . The modern state is increasingly anti-Christian, and its law structure is more and more humanistic and relativistic." [48]

Giving credit where credit is due, American law **was** long established in Biblical roots.

". . . Anglo-American jurisprudence has been very strongly grounded in a Biblical or moral view of the antithesis.

. . . . The relativists in the Western tradition still cling to, and are motivated by, a passion for justice which springs out of their Christian past, but their philosophy and action is leading to a radical disintegration of their causes. If good and evil are relative to man, then they are illusions as far as any objective validity is concerned. There is then no right nor wrong, but only the will of anarchistic man, or the superior will of the totalitarian state . . . .

This makes apparent why there is a legal and a moral crisis today. In the Anglo-American tradition of jurisprudence, the Biblical revelation has been decisive. The purpose of law is to codify and enforce the moral system of Biblical faith. The common law embodied this purpose. As Rowenstock-Huessy pointed out, 'Common Law was the product of a union between universal Christian laws and local customs.' This heritage was further developed by the adoption, in New England and other American colonies on a wholesale basis, of Biblical law directly from Scripture. The result was that the American

*tradition of jurisprudence was biblically rein-
forced at a time when the tradition was waning in
Britain.*

*After the Civil War, statute law rapidly took
over in America, and the background of this
statute law was the revelation imbibed from
European philosophies . . . .*[49]

*. . . . . The modern state is in-
creasingly anti-Christian, and its law structure is
more and more humanistic and relativistic."* [50]

A good example of this relativism is the differing
concept of law held by Gov. George Wallace and
Judge Frank Johnson, who both attended the same
law school.

It is important to realize that Russian intellectuals of
the prerevolutionary era totally adopted Western
humanistic and secular ideas. Hugh Seton-Watson
brought this to light in an article entitled, "The Russian
Intellectual," which appeared in the September, 1955
Encounter.[51]

*"As a result, 'The notion of law had little
meaning for them. They could not conceive that
the principle of the rule of law could be important.' Their idea was 'the reign of virtue on earth,'
and this reign meant the triumph of the intellectual and his ideas.*

*". . . The mind of the intellectual is seen as ul-
timate . . . . As a result, the intellectual, whether
Russian, Asiatic, African, or Western, sees his
thinking as basic to the idea of law. Law is what
humanistic man determines it to be when he
thinks in purely autonomous terms, without
reference to God. For the Russian, this has
meant direct rule and power; for the Western in-*

tellectual, it means the facade of legal tradition. In either case, law is what the autonomous mind of intellectual man says it is. As a result, the modern intellectual has applied his faith to the world as a new revelation of law with all the fervor of a god, who knows he is right . . . .

The new gods ruled divine justice, God's law, out of court. Henceforth, a new doctrine of justice came into being from the new gods of creation, social justice . . . .

This doctrine of social justice became a declaration of war against God, the church, the family, humanity, capitalism, and much more. How can capitalists fight a humanistic concept of justice which means injustice to them and which robs them, when they themselves are humanistic and have no regard for God's law?"[52]

Economics

Free enterprise **versus** State monitored and controlled economy

" 'When studied with any degree of thoroughness, the economic problem will be found to run into the political problem,' wrote Irving Babbitt, 'the political problem into the philosophical problem, and the philosophical problem itself to almost indissolubly bound up at last with the religious problem'.[53]

In short, what we believe or do not believe about man and about God determines what kind of society we will have and how our society will govern itself." [54]

"Indeed, economy is what it is because man is what he is. This being so, anyone attempting to institute new and different economic

178

arrangements must perforce also devise a new man, new society, new morality, and so on. It may be less painful to go about it gradually than in one fell swoop, but the damage must finally be done whichever way is taken. The damage must be done because the old man, the old society, the old morality, and so on, must be rooted out, altered, or destroyed." [55]

This is particularly true in today's world of specialization and sophisticated markets where there are few individuals or families who are self-sufficient with regard to their basic needs - food, water, shelter, clothing. Economics takes on a role of critical importance as man's relationship to "things" in integrated with, and precedes his relationship to other men (ethics).[56] Man's wants are endless. Resources are scarce. Economics is the study of how man chooses to utilize scarce resources.

*"There are two alternatives (basically different) principles on which society can be organized, (1) on the principle of coercion, or (2) on the principle of **contract** (voluntary cooperation).*

*The Hebrew-Christian religion, by the sixth commandment of the Decalogue, establishes a **contract society**, where people **agree** to a division of the proceeds, because they get a **benefit** from that division of the proceeds, or (to change the words) the distribution of the proceeds.*

*A **contract** society is a **just** society. A **coercive** society is an **unjust** society; it will not be necessary to be coercive, if there is **mutual** benefit — at least **some** benefit to both (or all) participants. The mutuality does not need to be*

equal *for a society to be a just society, but there* **must be** *mutuality.*"[57]

Thus, free enterprise is the Biblical view of economics. But economics, even free enterprise economics, fits **within** the overall Christian program. It is a part of a whole. Economics is not, from the Christian perspective, the focal issue in life. Materialism, accumulation, storing up of wealth on earth, is alien to Christianity. Jesus said, "Lay not up for yourselves treasures upon earth, where moth and rust doth corrupt, and where thieves break through and steal: But lay up for yourselves treasures in heaven, where neither moth and rust doth corrupt, and where thieves do not break through nor steal: For where your treasure is, there will your heart be also."[58] In fact, Jesus urged his disciples to, ". . . seek ye first the kingdom of God, and his righteousness; and all these things shall be added unto you."[59] Money and wealth, from the Christian perspective, is a false security. Man has a tendency to focus on himself, provide for his own security, with resultant pride, as opposed to focusing on God as the source of strength. That is why the Bible states, "For the love of money is the root of all evil: which while some coveted after, they have erred from the faith, and pierced themselves through with many sorrows."[60] From a Christian perspective, those that seek wealth are on the road to destruction. "But they that will be rich fall into temptation and a snare, and into many foolish and hurtful lusts, which drown men in destruction and perdition."[61] ". . . It is easier for a camel to go through the eye of a needle, than for a rich man to enter into the kingdom of God."[62] The undistorted Protestant ethic is to work hard, earn all one can, save all one can, and **give all one can.** Obviously, without this orientation, the doctrine of envy, which so prevades society today, becomes dominant. Entrepreneurs and businessmen under the warped, humanistic version of laissez faire have license to do whatever is necessary to accomplish their ends. Under this distortion, the modern businessman is not under the laws of God, and, is thus, under relativism. It should come as no surprise that the companion doctrine of caveat emptor (Let the buyer beware.) serves as justification for all types of non-Christian actions such as stock frauds, planned obsolescence, and misuse of resources in the lust to accumulate. But as the producers of society, businessmen have little time or use for much other than business. And so, reaping what they sow, the doctrine of greed and envy encompasses the intellectuals who can readily see that the businessman is, on the whole, not as bright as they are, and thus the intellectuals condemn the businessman under the guise of inequality in the distribution of wealth. They serve as the spokesmen of labor who are also envious and demand that government redistribute wealth. Thus, there is little wonder, as Schumpeter observed, that the success of capitalism will destroy itself. Capitalism, as practiced in the Western World, is unequivocally not Christian. Its goal is accumulation for self, not service to God. It is the breeding ground for greed, envy, theft, ruthless competition, and conflict. Underlying big business today is the unceasing conflict of the dialectic. The gods are materialism for the masses and growth for big business.

The Christian approach to economics is free enterprise, but not free enterprise which is based on the dialectic, and the pride and false security of accumulation. That leads to the conflict via the antithesis of labor and government. Rather, the Christian perspective is one of voluntary **service,** of it being better to give than receive, "And if any man will sue thee at the law, and take away thy coat, let him have thy cloak also. And whosoever shall compel thee to go a mile, go with him twain. Give to him that asketh thee, and from him that would borrow of thee turn not thou away."[63] "If thou wilt be perfect, go and sell that thou hast, and give it to the poor, and thou shalt have treasure in heaven: . . . ."[64] "It is more blessed to give than to receive."[65]

Adam Smith's unseen hand in the **Wealth of Nations** is the hand of God. Self-interest is best realized by service to fellow man (in free markets), not by being selfish. The successful businessman must give in order to receive. Success is built upon satisfying the needs of others, successful giving. If one thinks back to the most important persons in life, they are the ones who have given of themselves. The successful salesman heeds the needs of his clients. The successful doctor listens to his patient's complaints. He is others oriented. The entrepreneur fulfills a need of the public in the most efficient way possible.

Ruthless competition is not in evidence since, under the focus of service, the businessman is primarily interested in meeting the consumer's needs. **Competition** in the marketplace is a **secondary result** of different groups simultaneously seeking to meet society's requirements. It is not the focal issue, as it is under the dialectic. **It is** more blessed to give than receive, for by giving, one can best receive.

David Ricardo's Law of Cooperation and Association showed clearly the benefits of human interaction and sharing of tasks among **equally unequal** men under voluntary contract, free of coercion. A voluntary, contractual division of labor results in benefits to all. Meaning and happiness in life comes from voluntary association with others, as does economic prosperity.

The popular systems approach to business is based on the concept of synergy - the whole is greater than the sum of its parts. Thus, if one department maximizes its interests at the expense of the overall organization (suboptimization), the whole organization suffers. Maximum efficiency is achieved by **voluntary** cooperation toward an objective by all involved parties.

A quick look at some of the other problems stemming from a non-Christian concept of free enterprise is appropriate. From the Biblical viewpoint, debt is slavery, a status to be shunned. "Owe no man any thing . . . ."[66] Yet, the assumption of debt is common under capitalism, and today underlies the whole business structure. Debt today is a form of counterfeiting, and is insidious theft, for debt is achieved through the fractional reserve system, which results in the expansion of the money supply, which results in inflation as more money chases the same amount of goods. Therefore, those who get the money first-debtors, borrowers from the future-benefit unjustly at the expense of others for they get first shot at goods and services at the old prices. As the money becomes worth less, borrowers repay their loans with money of less value. This is insidious theft. Ultimately, the chickens come home to roost. Just as booms are caused by credit expansions, so are depressions created by credit contractions. As confidence subsides, businesses with excess inventories accumulated during the boom times must liquidate at a loss.

Dr. Hans F. Sennholz, head of the Department of Economics at Grove City College in Pennsylvania, put it thus, "The ultimate roots of the Great Depression were growing in the hearts and minds of the American people . . . the large majority favored and voted for the very policies that made the disaster inevitable: inflation and credit expansion, . . ."[67]

If one was not exposed to Western Civilization

business, but had a working understanding of the dialectic, one might **expect** business to take on a certain ruthlessness, much like a "king of the hill" child's game where, over time, a victor would emerge in the form of an octopus. This business organization could have been first expected to dominate in its field, from there expand to other areas nationally, and then internationally. (Businesses, for purposes here, include banks.) These organizations would necessarily be formed as corporations in order to enjoy protection under the questionable concept of limited liability.

In Chapter XVI, "The Inevitability of War: Hegel's Dialectic," the influence of Hegel, Darwin, and Spengler on big business was discussed. Also covered were some of the unethical and questionable business practices one might expect would result (and have resulted) from the relativism and ruthlessness of the dialectic. In addition to the practices listed there, one might also expect an advertising program geared to everlastingly fan the fire of consumers' endless wants by appealing to their pride, fear, or weaknesses. Such could be the tracks left, over time, by the "kings of the hill."

The target of the advertising, the workers, one might expect to be trapped in heavy debt, a form of slavery, where there would be little difference in status between them and the endentured servants or landlord/serf relationships of previous historical eras. One might expect the workers to emphasize leisure, job change, job absenteeism, job enrichment programs, and unions as a substitute for a sense of meaning and purpose in work. Violence, drugs, and mental illness could be expected as the logical result of workers spending two thirds of their waking hours in an endeavor which is seen as just "a necessary evil."

One might put the tag of multinationals on these giants, the result of the "survival of the fittest."

And what kind of life has resulted from the dialectic in business? Dr. E.F. Schumacher, author of **Small is Beautiful: Economics as if People Mattered,** has observed that growth economics is the religion of this age, and

"... *our neglect of the spiritual aspects of life in favor of the deification of material goods has eaten into our very substance. By so single-mindedly cultivating an ever-expanding greed and envy, we have debased ourselves .... We have destroyed our intelligence, happiness, and serenity.*

And we have done more yet. We've plundered and sacked and raped this planet's assets ...

.... I do not know which of these three increasingly insistent crises - human, environmental, or capital resource - is most likely to be the direct cause of our society's collapse. But I do know that a society which seeks fulfillment only in mindless material expansion does not fit into this world for long. There simply is no place for infinite growth on a finite planet .... [68]

.... In fact, in the Christian tradition, the doctrines of the Four Cardinal Virtues provide a marvelously subtle and realistic insight which is completely relevant and appropriate to the modern predicament in which we now find ourselves.

The Latin names of the Four Cardinal Virtues-prudentia, justitia, fortitudo, and temperantia-denote rather higher orders of

*human excellence than their English derivatives
... but we can see at once that those derivatives
are prudence, justice, fortitude, and
temperance."* [69]

Schumacher went on to say,

> *"The technology of the modern world is
> utterly steeped in a violence of the most ap-
> palling magnitude. And this violence is just as
> apparent in what we call 'peace' as it is in war.
> [The dialectic can only work this way.]*
>
> *There is absolutely no limit to the violence
> that modern man will permit himself in the name
> of 'peaceful economic progress.' ... We rip the
> earth apart, turn it upside down, and ruin it for
> all time with ever-bigger machines for the sake
> of the same immediate, and fleeting, profits. We
> increasingly brutalize and debase even
> ourselves-eliminate the joy from our work, turn
> ourselves into mere machine tenders, and sur-
> round ourselves with ugliness, intolerable noise,
> and fear of the future - all in the name of
> progress."* [70]

Dr. Schumacher felt that Thomas Aquinas, the
great Christian Saint, summed up what society's outlook on life should be in **The Foundation.**

> *" 'Man was created to praise, reverence, and
> serve God our Lord, and by this means, to save
> his soul.*
>
> *And the other things on the face of the earth
> were created for man's sake, and in order to aid
> him in the prosecution of the end for which he
> was created.*
>
> *From whence it follows that man ought to make*

use of them just so far as they help him to attain his end.

And that he ought to withdraw himself from them just so far as they hinder him.' " [71]

Heilbroner attacks Western capitalism in much the same manner. He states that capitalism had always been justified on the grounds that happiness and material goods went hand in hand. Today, Americans have plenty of material goods. But how much happier, wiser, or more at peace are they than their ancestors? Money is not a substitute for other values. Work is an end in itself. Today the quality of personal production is ignored. On these counts also the defense of dialectical capitalism fails.[72] Heilbroner declares,

"No other civilization has permitted the calculus of selfishness to so dominate its lifeways, nor has any other civilization allowed this narrowest of all motivations to be elevated to the status of a near categorical imperative.[73]

.... I suspect that a major force for the transformation of business civilization will be a new religious orientation, directed against the canons and precepts of our time, and oriented toward a wholly different conception of the meaning of life and a mode of social organization congenial to the encouragement of that life." [74]

It has been taken for granted here that regardless of all its faults, there is no disputing the fact that Western free enterprise has outproduced the state controlled economic systems, whether communistic or socialistic, both humanistic. In the U.S.S.R., the incredibly large percentage of food that is raised in private plots allowed the peasants illustrates the point clearly. The largest Soviet domestic propaganda agency, the **Znaniye,** reported that 37 million families in the U.S.S.R. have private garden plots of less than one half acre per family. That represents less than 1.5% of all the farmed land in the Soviet Union. The garden plots, however, accounted for 61% of the potatoes, 34% of the vegetables, and 40% of the fruits raised in the U.S.S.R. Additionally, 22.5% of the cattle, 18.9% of the hogs, 21% of the sheep and goats, and 52.7% of the poultry raised in the Soviet Union were raised in the private gardens. Economic freedom results in production.[75] Where there is no freedom there is no abundant production, only shortages.

Economics comes down to religion. As Clarence B. Carson put it clearly in his work, "World in the Grip of an Idea",

> *"Marxism . . . is an anti-religious religion. It is an earthbound, materialistic, man centered, cataclysmic, prophetic, and dogmatic religion. Dialectical materialism is its revelation. History is its god. Marx is its prophet. Lenin is its incarnation. The revolution is its day of judgment. And communism is its paradise. Its claim to being scientific even satisfies the intellectual's desire to have a rational religion."* [76]

That Marxism is a religion is rather well known. It was not widely realized however, that Western Civilization's economic system is based on the same dialectic which underlies the communist's economies. The respected American observer and philosopher, Alexis de Tocqueville, stated, " 'There are, at present, two great nations in the world, which started from different points but seem to tend toward the same end. I allude to the Russians and Americans.' "[77] The entire world's economic system is presently in conflict with God's laws. Mr. Carter, who is in the thick of involvement with big international business, is a flagrant violator.

Basic Christianity Today - A Nonentity

Today, the majority of modern churches are openly humanistic. Their humanism is couched in the term, "social action." This is the creed of the World Council of Churches as well as the National Council of Churches. Mr. Carter, however, belongs to that dwindling minority known as basic Christians. But by far, even those who march under this banner might as well put their staff in the closet. The basic Christian church, for the most part, has retreated into an inbred cocoon of self-righteousness, supposedly justified under the "doctrine of separation." (". . . whosoever therefore will be a friend of the world is the enemy of God." James 4:4). Wrongly applied, the "doctrine of separation" today is a leaking umbrella held by basic Christians seeking to escape from a world beyond their comprehension. Also, insidiously distorting the doctrine of grace by humanistically doing their "own thing," and ignoring the doctrine of works, they are content to study the Bible for self-contained "personal edification." Educated in the humanistic public school system, like the rest of society, they are mentally split, intellectually schizophrenic. Most are not even aware of the battle of opposites that is taking place in their own mind, much less how to relate or apply their doctrine to the rest of the "unbelieving world." Their "witnessing efforts" are often ineffectual since they are unaware that the difference in presuppositions is so great, it is like talking to a stranger in a foreign language. They are, for the most part, traditional drones hanging on to a raveling thread of security. The concept of truth applied, and the power inherent in such, is alien to them. Mr. Carter could very well be counted in this group. Naive is an understatement for their condition.

The Vast Intellectual Majority

What is frightening is the fact that there is no meaningful army anywhere today in the world to counteract the ever increasing, slashing, destructive onslaught of humanism. There is simply no balance of power. The unified family of relativism and humanism, clothed in the necessary conflict of Hegel's dialectic, opens the door for the war cycles about to descend upon mankind. The reason for the spread of communism, and now the growing anarchy and rebellion against government, is no mystery. It is simply the result of humanism filling a vacuum of unbelief.

In the long run, this might be a blessing for humanity. A market saturated with buyers collapses under its own weight. Humanism should also collapse under its own weight, particularly when one considers that the saturation of humanism is totally underpinned by conflict. One must be philosophical here. The next 6-20 years the violence and misery could be ghastly. But for those who are around in 2006, it should again be calm. By then, the cycle from mobocracy to Caesar should have run its course and a glimmer of freedom reappear.

A twenty year problem is not a short-term problem. The world is apparently about to move from a long period (approximately 30 years) of ease through a long time of great difficulty (20 years). The last thing it needs is to sail the rough, shark-infested waters on the leaking and unstable raft of humanism.

If ever the United States needed to pull together, it is now. If ever the United States needed a President who understood the real problems, who was farsighted, who was consistent to his beliefs, who would lead the people in a direction where they are now inclined to turn, it is now. The people of the United States sense immense danger ahead, and rightly so. They are alienated from an irrevelant government that is acting like a bunch of cowboys the first time at sea, chewing tobacco while the civilization crushing tidal wave approaches.

Carter's Minority (Intellectual) Support

An abrupt change in direction by Mr. Carter should make some difference. It would take such a move in order to slowly turn the people of the United States from the potentially destructive path.

Granted, there is not enough time for all that needs to be done, even if alterations began tomorrow. And unfortunately, people resist change. Change comes slowly, very slowly, or very abruptly and painfully. The stage is set for a good dose of the latter. Mr. Carter does have some intellectual support for his presuppositions.

William Rees-Mogg, editor of **The London Times,** wrote in his book, **The Crisis of World Inflation,**

"All religions involve a spiritual order for believers. Any man who believes in God believes in a spiritual authority other than himself, and infinitely more important than himself. His spiritual universe is one in which he is a very small and remote moon reflecting the light of an infinitely great sun, cherished and warmed by the sun, but smaller than any grain of sand beside it.

So long as he adheres to this belief . . . a sanity [is] imposed upon him. He cannot see himself as inordinately important . . . .

As religion has declined this has been an age in which men proclaimed themselves gods. How many gods we have seen: Benito Mussolini, Adolf Hitler, Joseph Stalin, Charles Manson, Idi Amin, and the Eastern gods, gods of all races. One thing they all have in common. They are all killers and they are all mad, all filled with the mythical sense of their own godhood, of their own supreme importance. . . .

It is all madness. And one can see the logic of this madness. There is no god; therefore there is no personality with authority over my personality; therefore my personality is unlimited; but there are people who oppose my will; therefore they are wicked; . . . therefore they must be destroyed, liquidated, there must be a final solution; only those who appreciate my superordinate quality are fit to live in our new world of Nazism/Fascism/Soviet Communism. Everyone else is a traitor. This is the logic of megalomania, most dangerous when it is pushed to the level of self-apotheosis.

This too is found in history. The Roman emperors went mad by the dozen; . . . . But to this grand folly, which is itself so conspicuous in our own century, there is the counterpart, a lesser, commoner madness, which affects millions. That is the madness not of the human god, but of the worshipper at the shrine of humanity." [78]

Respected historian Arnold Toynbee observed, " 'It will be hard indeed to refill the spiritual vacuum which is being hollowed in our western hearts by the progressive decay of religious beliefs.' "[79] After years of research, in 1939, Toynbee switched radically from a view of civilizations as the basic unit of society to a view which held that religion was the basic unit of society. Toynbee felt,

> "The decline of the West certainly seems inevitable according to the pattern of the past. Modern technology, the prospects of a third world war, the possibility of a 'great famine,' and original sin in man make prognostications rather bleak. However, there is the possibility that Western man may yet turn to Religion as his means of glorifying God and enjoying Him once again. According to Toynbee, this is the only essence of deliverance from destruction." [80]

In **Civilization on Trial,** Toynbee declared, "With God's help, man is master of his own destiny, at least to some extent in some respects."[81] Just a short time before his death, his last major work appeared entitled, **Mankind and Mother Earth: A Narrative History of the World.** There he stated that religion is "the most important of all human experiences."[82]

The French social critic, Jacques Ellul, stated in **The New Demons** that contemporary man is as religious as his ancestors, but the vacuum of unbelief by the "death of God" has been filled by the gods of politics and technology. "Ellul repeatedly insists that only faith in Jesus Christ, whose kingdom is not of this world, can save mankind."[83]

The French historian, Amaury de Riencourt, noted,

> "Intimacy, familiarity, lack of reverence have become the dominant themes of American life. Nothing leads more implacably to Caesarism than these traits. The democratic idea that any man is as good as his neighbor automatically destroys the vital tension, the desire to emulate and 'reach up to.' Even when practiced with as

much engaging friendliness as in America, its main result is to nip in the bud any form of self-improvement. The iron-willed Puritan was accustomed to raise his eyes to God, look at Him with reverence and, in his striving, become more spiritualized. His modern descendants have lowered their sights and look horizontally at the 'common man'. The steady process of humanizing and vulgarizing has destroyed a great deal of vital and creative tension." [84]

Riencourt also stated,

". . . the Messianic notion that the process of Time had metaphysical significance, that history had a meaning, the apocalyptic notion of Revelation, of the Prophet who sees God not merely in Eternity but also in Time, not merely in nature's universe but in the very process of man's history. All prophetic creeds saw in the historical development of mankind the most profound revelation of Divine Wisdom; and it was in Christianity that this revolutionary outlook eventually assumed its full dimensions, in the idea of Christ as the hinge between Time and Eternity. Christ became the concrete manifestation of Eternity in History, of the Timeless in Time. In the words of the Bible, "When the fullness of time was come, God sent forth his Son.' " [85]

Implications For Freedom

State domination, followed by war and anarchy, followed by Caesar, seems to be the wave of the future. There is no room for a passenger called freedom. The **Chalcedon Report** for September 1977 stated,

"In fact, as George Orwell saw, the new

slavery comes in the name of freedom. People talk of freedom, equality, social justice, and brotherhood while busily voting in their opposite . . . .

. . . . Freedom and justice will rise and fall in terms of man's faith. Where men are regenerate and live in terms of God's law, freedom and justice quickly become imperatives. Where men are reprobate, the facade of freedom and justice becomes basic to the New Slavery. A faith without consequences is no faith at all." [86]

There is great depth to the statement, "And ye shall know the truth, and the truth shall set you free."[87]

Carter's Discipline?

Mr. Carter's God, the God of the **Bible,** has a habit of disciplining members of His family. Hebrews 12:6 declares, "For whom the Lord loveth he chasteneth, and scourgeth every son whom he receiveth." This is known as the Christian doctrine of discipline for learning, discipline for growth in the Christian life. God's love, however, always allows grace to precede discipline, i.e., the guilty son has an opportunity to repent.

Mr. Carter is not keeping the laws of his God. More condemning is the fact that Mr. Carter is sponsoring and carrying out programs and policies that are anathema to Him. Perhaps Mr. Carter's plight is like King Saul's, King of Israel, in the Old Testament.

King Saul was the Lord's anointed king. The Lord sent Saul out to utterly destroy Amalek and all that he had including, ". . . both man and woman, infant and suckling, ox and sheep, camel and ass."[88] But upon the people insistence (humanism), Saul violated the Lord's commandment and spared, ". . . the best of the sheep, and of the oxen, and of the fatlings, and the lambs, and all that was good, . . ."[89] (Apparently then, as now, people, under humanism, account for little.) As a result of his disobedience, the Lord rejected Saul as King of Israel. From then on, it was all downhill for Saul. The inglorious conclusion to Saul's life was in battle on Mount Gilboa where the Philistines were fighting against Israel. First, the Philistines killed the sons of Saul - Jonathan, Abinadab, and Malchischua. Then, archers wounded Saul. Next, Saul fell on his own sword (suicide). The Philistines cut off Saul's head and fastened his body, along with the bodies of his three sons, to the wall of Bethshan.[90]

Mr. Carter will be up for possible reelection in 1980. He should recall the fact that every President elected on a "0" year in this country since 1840 has died in office. In light of his flagrant violation of his God's laws, perhaps Mr. Carter should spend some serious time on his knees.

The Jaycee Creed

The Creed of the U.S. Junior Chamber of Commerce perfectly illustrate the inconsistency and conflict inherent in the United States today. It is as follows:

"WE BELIEVE:
That faith in God gives meaning and purpose to human life:"
So far so good. Authority is established. A firm presuppositional foundation is laid.

"That the brotherhood of man transcends the sovereignty of nations;"
Sounds good, but the concept of the brotherhood of man today is the best manifestation of humanism one can think of. It is used as the excuse for all kinds of

worldwide atrocities, including massacres of innocent children, other acts of terrorism, violation of property rights, and on and on. Humanism inevitably lead to the tyranny of man over man. Nations, in turn, are from a Biblical perspective, established for the protection of man. Nations establish a balance of power, and thus tend to counteract the corruption which comes with absolute power, and the deification of the Caesar or the State. Nations are for the protection of man when they function under their limited duty of providing for the defense, and insuring justice under divine law.

"That economic justice can best be won by free men through free enterprise;"

Absolutely, if free enterprise is also under law, which throws out the relativism of laissez faire and caveat emptor.

"That government should be of laws rather than of men;"

O.K. If men don't establish laws then a God must.

"That earth's great treasure lies in human personality; and That service to humanity is the best work of life."

No argument there. Marx, Lenin, and Mao all agree, at least in theory. But the source of decision for this service must be individual, for coercion by man over man leads to collective human misery.

Man's Need For Stability

The human organism needs stability. The natural universe has unpleasant and unexpected occurrences - hailstorms, tornadoes, drought, disease, death - just to name a few, which easily upset the emotional stability of man. Thus, man has enough difficulties without the added burden of human instability. When the natural crises hit, it is important for man to have a stable base to fall back on. The added disadvantage of human instability (Hegel's dialectic and humanism), coupled with man's propensity for violence, can multiply misery many times.

Maslow, in his hierarchy of needs, concluded that man's basic needs are biological and then safety. Thinking in terms of analogy, which is theistic in nature as it assumes a divine integrator, the biological system of man needs stability. It requires regular rest, exercise, protection from harsh elements, and timely nutrition in order to function at maximum efficiency over an extended period of time.

The mind of man needs stability if it is to avoid maladies over time in the form of mental illness or psychosomatic difficulties. The love, security, safety, and stability of the home has been consistently recognized as the basic building block of society. When the home disintegrates, the society fails. Psychologists have observed that the mental and emotional stability of children is established in the years from birth to age six, while the child is at home.

Nations have historically required stable money in order to maintain a healthy society. Even John Maynard Keynes, who is assailed by conservatives as the author of world inflation, advocated an international gold standard. In the March 20, 1933, **Economist,** Keynes stated his attitude toward gold. " 'At all stages of the post-war developments the concrete proposals which I have brought forward from time to time have been based on the use of gold as an international standard, whilst discarding it as a rigid national standard.' "[91] Today, inflation, the seemingly inevitably handmaiden of an unstable currency, is destroying the foundation of civilization.

As stated previously, good results are the product of correct thinking. Correct thinking is the result of accurate assumptions on the nature of life, correct presuppositions. Stable presuppositions, which come home to roost in the antithesis, opposites, and absolutes are unavoidably, by their very nature, theistic. The concept of an integrating God who is omniscient, omnipresent, and omnipotent provides the stability necessary for man. It is the only possibility whereby man can rationally relate to his universal environment.

Today, the world's thinking can be pictured as a spiral down, with the beasts of relativism, humanism, socialism, communism, and all the other offshoots energized by the instability and conflict of Hegel's dialectic. The dialectic makes conflict inevitable, and under humanism and relativism, war is justified for any reason.

The cycles of war are about to descend upon man. If they are inspected closely, it becomes obvious that they are, for the most part, created by man directly. War is an historical and integral part of human nature. As Toynbee declared, " 'The institute of war lies close to the heart of mankind.' "[92] Cycles of war predict a constant, human nature. The erudite W.D. Gann stated it clearly, "TIME CYCLES repeat because human nature does not change. That is why wars occur at regular CYCLES."[93]

The dialectic is insidious. It grips men of all classes, ages, intellect, and races. It has placed in irreconcilable conflict the leader of the free world. It all comes down, however, to the antithesis. Man fights the battle between pride and humility. Humility leads to the edification of man. Pride goeth before a fall. The decision, on faith, to be subservient to God is an act of humility. The decision, on faith, to be a man-god is an act of pride. As a man thinketh, so he is.[94] Century after century, man fights this same battle. Sagacious old Copernicus would smile. He knows the fight. Man is still not the center of the universe.

To break the power of the war cycles requires an individual decision, a change of mind, a reorientation to God and God's laws as a necessary first step. While synergistically, the whole may be greater than the sum of its parts, it is necessarily composed of its parts. Thus, any collective action must begin with "me". An ancient Oriental Maxim states this beautifully:

" 'If there is righteousness in the heart
 there will be beauty in the character
If there is beauty in the character
 there will be harmony in the family home
If there is harmony in the home
 there will be order in the nation
When there is order in the nation
 there will be peace in the world.' "[95]

Notes and References

CHAPTER I

1. Bill Peterson, **The Last Days of Man** (New York: Warner Books, Inc., 1977) p. 100, quoting Arnold Toynbee's **A Study of History.**
2. Karl Von Clausewitz, **On War** (New York: Random House, Inc., 1943) p. 3.
3. Ibid., p. 16.

CHAPTER II

1. David C. McClelland, "Love and Power; The Psychological Signals of War," **Psychology Today,** (January 1975), p. 44.
2. Ibid.
3. Ibid., p. 47.
4. Ibid.
5. Jack Mabley, "A Worry or A Warning," **Chicago Tribune,** October 12, 1977.
6. Ibid.
7. McClelland, op. cit., p. 46.

CHAPTER III

1. Julian M. Snyder, **International Moneyline,** (November 1976), 16 East Trail, Darien, Connecticut 06820.
2. Harry D. Schultz, **The International Harry Schultz Letter,** No. 368, (May 1977), p. 6., P.O. Box 2523, Lausanne 1002, Switzerland.
3. William Rees - Mogg, **The Crisis of World Inflation** (Greenwich, Conn: Baxter World Economic Service, 1975) p. 50.
4. Ibid., pp. 66-67.
5. Freidrich A. Hayek, "Toward Free Market Money," **The Wall Street Journal,** August 19, 1977, p. 10.

6. Snyder, op. cit.

7. L.J. Jensen, **Astrocycles and Speculative Markets** (Pomeroy, Washington: Lambert Gann Publishing Co., 1978) p. 12.

8. Ibid., p. 17.

9. Max Gunter, **Wall Street and Witchcraft** (New York: Bernard Geis Associates, 1971) pp. 66-67.

10. Jack Sauers, "Letters," **Cycles,** Vol. XXVIII, No. 1, (January 1977), p. 21.

CHAPTER IV

1. Nels Winkless III and Iben Browning, **Climate and the Affairs of Men** (New York: Harper's Magazine Press, 1975) p. 17.

2. "World Weather: Ominous Changes Ahead?", **The Morgan Guaranty Survey,** (March 1977), p. 6.

3. Winkless and Browning, op. cit., p. 17.

4. Ibid., p. 157.

5. Ibid., pp. 170-185.

6. Ibid. p. 191.

7. Ibid p. 213.

8. Edward R. Dewey with Og Mandino, **Cycles, The Mysterious Forces That Trigger Events** (New York: Manor Books, Inc., 1973) pp. 136-138.

9. Ibid., pp. 138-139.

10. Ibid., p. 138.

11. Ellsworth Huntington, **Mainsprings of Civilization** (New York: John Wiley and Sons, Inc., 1945) p. 489.

12. Dewey and Mandino, op. cit., p. 150.

13. Ibid., p. 151.

14. Bernard Fremerman, "Cyclical Phenomena," **Cycles,** Vol. XXVIII, No. 2, (Feb-Mar 1977), p. 44.

15. Ibid., p. 44.

16. Ibid., p. 45.

17. Ibid.

18. Herb Rogers, "Planetary Influences on the Earth," Lecture Series at Wheatridge Baptist Church, Denver, Colorado, July 20, 1975.

19. Ibid.

20. Ibid.

21. D. Modin, **Prophecy 1973-2000** (Los Angeles: Hermes House, 1972), p. 157.

22. Ibid., p. 137.

23. Robert H. Olsen, **The Final Years** (Santa Fe Springs, California: Stockton Trade Press, Inc., 1973), pp. 30-31.

24. Ibid., p. 38.

25. Ibid., p. 39.

26. Ibid.

27. Ibid.

28. Gertrude Shirk, "Cycles In Ice Ages," **Cycles,** Vol. 28, No. 3, (Apr-May 1977), p. 63.

29. Ibid., p. 62.

30. Olsen, op. cit., p. 38.

CHAPTER V

1. "Commodity Chart Service," Commodity Research Bureau, One Liberty Plaza, New York, N.Y., 10006.

2. Ludwig von Mises, **Human Action,** (Chicago: Henry Regnery Company, 1966), p. 824.

3. Ibid., p. 831.

4. Dewey and Mandino, op. cit., p. 157.

5. Ann McFealters, **"Americans Warned of Water Crisis," The Rocky Mountain News,** April 24, 1975, p. 24.

6. Ibid.

7. Thomas O'Toole, "Over 40% of World's Food Is Lost to Pests", **The Washington Post,** Feb. 13, 1977, p. E-2.

8. "Blueprint for Debate on "Hunger," **The Spokesman-Review,** June 26, 1977, Finance Section.

9. Dr. Reid Bryson, "The Plowboy Interview," **The Mother Earth News,** No. 38, (March 1976), p. 12.

10. Ibid., p. 12-13.

11. Frederick G. Uhlmann, 'Commodity Commentary" Drexel Burnham Lambert No. 34, Sept. 12, 1977, 20 Broad Street, New York, NY 10004.

12. "Living in the Shadow of Worldwide Famine," **The Plain Truth,** (February 1977), p. 42.

13. C.V. Myers, "The Unimaginable Catastrophe," **Myers Finance and Energy,** No. 247, p. 4., (May 27, 1977), 642 Peyton Building, Spokane, WA 99201.

14. Ibid., p. 5.

15. Ibid., p. 6.

16. Ibid., p. 7.

17. Jai-Hoon Yang "The Nature and Origins of the U.S. Energy Crisis," **Review,** Vol. 59, No. 7, (July 1977), p. 2., Federal Reserve Bank of St. Louis.

18. Ibid., p. 12.

19. Myers, op. cit., p. 7.

20. Peterson, op. cit., pp. 15-16.

21. Ibid., p. 106.

22. Ibid.

CHAPTER VI

1. Kenneth O. Gangel, "Arnold Toynbee. The Man and His Message", **Bibliotheca Sacra,** Vol. 134 No. 533, (Jan-Mar 1977), p. 53.

2. Ibid. p. 56.

3. Ibid., quoting Toynbee, **A Study of History,** abridgement by Somervell, 1: 578.

4. Ibid.

5. Ibid.

6. Ibid., p. 57.

7. "Foundation Reprint No. 7," **Foundation for the Study of Cycles,** 124 S. Highland Drive, Pittsburgh, Penn. 15206, 1944, p. 7, reprinting Edwin Franden Dakin, "Introduction," **Today and Destiny** (New York: Alfred A. Knopf) 1940.

8. Ibid., pp. 12-13.

9. Ibid., p. 15.

10. Ibid.

11. Amaury De Riencourt, **The Coming Caesars,** (New York: Coward-McCann, Inc., 1957) pp. 10-11.

12. Ibid., pp. 241-242.

13. Ibid., p. 354.

14. Ibid., p. 355.

15. Ibid., p. 356.

16. Ibid., p. 352.

17. Ibid., p. 353.

18. Peterson, op. cit., p. 100.

19. Ibid.

CHAPTER VII

1. Roberto Vacca, **The Coming Dark Age,** (New York: Anchor Books, 1974) p. 4.

2. Ibid., p. 4.

3. Peterson, op. cit., p. 90.

4. Ibid.

5. Ibid., p. 89.

6. "Study Notes 'Parent Power' Declines, Urges Changes," **The Spokesman-Review",** September 11, 1977, p. A 23.

7. Peterson, op. cit., pp. 58-59.

8. Ibid., p. 61.

9. Howard J. Ruff, **The Ruff Times,** "Special Report #43," (September 1976), pp. 2-3, Target Publishers, P.O. Box 172, Alamo, Ca. 94507.

10. Ibid., pp. 4-9.

11. Ibid., p. 9.

12. Ibid., p. 13.

13. Ibid., p. 13.

14 Liz Roman Gallese, 'The Green Dream," **The Wall Street Journal,** Vol. LVII, No. 217, August 18, 1977, p. 1.

CHAPTER VIII

1. "Profile on An Aging America," **U.S. News and World Report,** August 8, 1977, p. 54.

2. Hugh P. King, "How It Came Out," "Hunter's Cycles of Optimism and Pessimism," **Cycles,** Vol. 26, No. 2, (March, 1975), p. 49. 124 South Highland Avenue, Pittsburgh, Pennsylvania 15206.

3. R. N. Elliott, **Nature's Law,** Chapter 15, p. 40, N.Y. City Public Library.

4. Dewey and Mandino, op. cit., p. 97.

5. **Cycle Sciences Corporation Newsletter,** October 1, 1976, 274 Brannon St., San Francisco, Ca. 94107.

6. Bob McGregor, "The Key to Understanding Market Movements" **World Money Analyst,** (August 15, 1977), p. 1, 1914 Asian House, One Hennessy Road, Hong Kong.

7. Norman Alcock, "Cyclical Analysis of Global Economy," **Cycles,** Vol. 28, No. 4, (June, 1977), p. 77.

8. Tom Wicker, "Carter: No . . ." International Syndicated Columnist.

9. Derek Reveron, "To Black Leaders Moral Drift Is a Big Problem," **The Wall Street Journal,** August 19, 1977, p. 10.

10. Ibid.

11. Ibid.

12. Modin, op. cit., p. 97.

13. McGregor, op. cit., p. 1.

CHAPTER IX

1. Snyder, op. cit., Reproducing the Kondratieff Wave from Media General **Financial Weekly,** P.O. Box 26991, Richmond, Va. 23621, August 1972.

2. "Growing Worry Over World Trade War," **U.S. News and World Report,** August 8, 1977, p. 24.

3. Ibid.

4. Alfred L. Malabre, Jr., "Trade Trouble," The Wall Street Journal, August, 11, 1977, p. 1.

5. "Trade War Jitters," The Plain Truth, (June, 1977), p. 4.

6. Ibid.

7. Ibid.

8. Von Mises, op. cit., p. 687.

9. Ibid., p. 832.

10. "Defining Rights," The Wall Street Journal, August 19, 1977, p. 10.

11. James B. Shuman and David Rosenau, The Kondratieff Wave, (New York: Dell Publishing Co., Inc., 1972), p. 157-161.

12. Elliott, op. cit., Chapters 1 & 2.

13. "Fibonacci Notes," Lambert-Gann Publishing Company, Box O, Pomeroy, Washington 99347.

14. Ibid.

For further study of the Kondratieff Wave :
The Donald J. Hoppe Analysis Vol. 1, No. 2, Feb. 20, 1976
Box 513
Crystal Lake, Il. 60014
        and
Richard Russell's Dow Theory Letters, Inc., No. 692, Mar. 18, 1977
P.O. Box 1759
LaJolla, California 92038

CHAPTER X

1. Winkless and Browning, op. cit., p. 161.

2. Kenneth H. Bacon, "Achilles' Heel," The Wall Street Journal, Vol. LVII, No. 210, August 9, 1977, p. 1.

3. "Illiteracy a Problem in Military," The Rocky Mountain News, March 21, 1977, p. 26.

4. "Collins Report Suppressed," Review of the News, August 31, 1977, p. 60.

5. "Soviet Submarine Missle Range Boosted to 5,750 Miles," The Rocky Mountain News, March 25, 1977, p. 19.

6. "U.S. Defense Cutback," Daily News Digest, Vol. 3, No. 46, September 7, 1977, p. 5, quoting Intelligence Digest Weekly

Review, August 24, 1977, London, Eng. (Daily News Digest, P.O. Box 27496, Phoenix, Arizona 85061).

7. Ibid.

8. Peter Arnett and Fred S. Hoffman, "Is America Ready to Fight a Conventional War," **Great FallsTribune,** September 26, 1977, p. 2.

9. Ibid.

10. James Sibbet, "Let's Talk . . . Silver and Gold," (May 20, 1977), p. 1. Sibbet Publications, 380 E. Green Street, Financial Building, S-200, Pasadena, Ca. 91101.

11. "U.S. Madness-Civil Defense," **Daily News Digest,** Vol. 3, No. 44, (August 24, 1977), p. 3, quoting **Albuquerque Journal,** August 12, 1977, p. G-4.

12. Lloyd Shearer, "Intelligence Report," **Parade,** (September 11, 1977), p. 10.

13. Dr. Harry D. Schultz, "Target America," **Exodus,** No. 23 (July 1977), p. 3, SOS, P.O. Box 7032, 4000 Dusseldorf 1, Germany.

14. "Soviet Missle Subs." **Daily News Digest,** Vol. 3, No. 45 (August 31, 1977), p. 7, quoting **Defense and Foreign Affairs Digest,** August 1977.

CHAPTER XI

1. Burton H. Pugh, **Trader's Instruction Book** (Pomeroy, Washington: Lambert-Gann Publishing Co., 1929) pp. 49-50.

2. Peterson, op. cit., pp. 29-36.

3. Matthew 25:13

4. "America Burned and Invaded," Gospel Tract Society, Inc., P.O. Box 1118, Independence, Mo.

5. Modin, op. cit., pp. 100-102.

6. Ibid., p. 121.

7. Ibid., pp. 148-149.

CHAPTER XII

1. "Gann Manuscripts," Lambert Gann Publishing Co., Rickman Gulch, Pomeroy, Washington.

2. Ibid.

3. Ibid.

CHAPTER XIII

1. Winkless and Browning, op. cit., p. 155.
2. Oswald Spengler, **The Decline of the West,** (New York: Alfred A. Knopf, Inc., 1922) p. 434.
3. Rene Baxter, **The Freedom Fighter,** Vol. 3, No. 14, (July 27, 1977), p. 2, quoting Dr. Harry D. Schultz, **The International Harry Schultz Letter.**
4. Ibid.
5. Ibid.
6. Ibid.
7. Riencount., op. cit., p. 164.
8. Ibid., p. 149.
9. Ibid., pp. 264-265.
10. Ibid., p. 253.
11. Ibid., p. 150, quoting Alexis de Tocqueville, **Democracy In America,** i, p. 413.
12. Elmer Pendell, **Why Civilizations Self-Destruct,** (Cape Canaveral; Howard Allen Enterprises, Inc., 1977) pp. 102-117.
13. Ibid., Inside front cover.
14. Ibid., p. 157.
15. Alan L. Otten, "Politics and People (Errand Boys)," **The Wall Street Journal,** August 18, 1977, Editorial Page.
16. Gary North, "Confessions of a Washington Reject," **Remnant Review,** Vol. IV, No. 16, (August 19, 1977), pp. 98-99. 713 Cornwallis Road, S-100, Durham, North Carolina 27707
17. Ibid., p. 99.
18. Ibid., p. 102.

CHAPTER XIV

1. Gary North, "National Emergencies and Confiscation," **Remnant Review,** Vol. III, No. 16, (August 18, 1976), p. 94.
2. Ibid., p. 95.
3. Ibid., pp. 96-100.

4. Howard J. Ruff, "That Strange Man," **The Ruff Times,** Vol. 3, Issue 16, (August 1, 1977), p. 3.

5. Ibid., pp. 3-4.

6. Murray N. Rothbard, "The Conspiracy Theory of History Revisited," **Reason,** (April 1977), p. 39.

7. Ibid.

8. Ibid.

9. Ibid.

10. Ibid.

11. Christopher Lydon, "Carter Revealed: He's A Rockefeller Republican," **The Atlantic Monthly,** Vol. 240, No. 1, (July, 1977), p. 55.

12. Ibid., p. 56.

13. Jeremiah Novak, "The Trilateral Connection," **The Atlantic Monthly,** Vol. 240, No. 1, (July, 1977), p. 57.

14. Ibid.

15. "The Trilateral Commission," **Parade, The Rocky Mountain News,** April 17, 1977, p. 14.

16. Novak, op. cit., p. 57.

17. Ibid., p. 58.

18. Ibid.

19. Ibid.

20. Ibid.

21. Dr. Harvey D. Schultz, **The International Harry Schultz Letter,** No. 373, p. 3, quoting **The Phoenix Gazette,** July 4, 1977, p. A7

22. Novak, op. cit., p. 58.

23. Ibid.

24. Ibid., p. 59.

25 Ibid.

26. Craig S. Karpel, "Cartergate: The Death of Democracy," **Penthouse,** Vol. 9, No. 3, (November, 1977), pp. 69-70.

27. Ibid., p. 69.

28. Ibid., p. 90.

29. Ibid.

30. Ibid., p. 104.

31. Ibid., p. 106.

32. Modin, op. cit., p. 72.

33. Ibid.

34. North, "National Emergencies and Confiscation," **Remnant Review,** op. cit., p. 95.

35. Ibid., p. 96.

36. Ibid., p. 97.

37. Ibid., pp. 97-98.

38. Ibid., pp. 98-99.

39. Patrick Wood, **Profiting From Uncertainty,** (Scottsdale, Arizona: The August Corp., 1977), pp. 13-14. The August Corp., P.O. Box 4218, Scottsdale, Arizona 85258.

CHAPTER XV

1. Richard Russell's, **Dow Theory Letters,** No. 691, (March 9, 1977), p. 6.

2. "A Thin-Skinned Jimmy Carter Comes Into Public View," U.S. **News and World Report,** August 29, 1977, p. 16.

CHAPTER XVI

1. Francis A. Shaeffer, **The God Who Is There,** (Downers Grove, Illinois: Inter-Varsity Press, 1969), pp. 14-20.

2. Ibid., p. 20.

3. John Warwick Montgomery, **Where Is History Going?,** (Grand Rapids: Zondervan Publishing House, 1969), p. 19.

4. Ibid.

5. John Kenneth Galbraith, "The Age of Uncertainty," Public Television.

6. Riencourt, op. cit., p. 179.

7. Lawrence Dennis, **The Dynamics of War and Revolution,** (The United States of America: The Weekly Foreign Letter, 1940), p. 64.

8. Ibid., p. 77.

9. Ibid., pp. 79-80.

10. Ibid., p. 81.

11. Stephen D. Krasner, "Why Multinationals Are Loved So Little," **The Wall Street Journal,** August 3, 1977, Editorial Page.

12. Von Mises, op. cit., p. 832.

13. Ibid., p. 686.

14. Ibid., p. 687.

15. Robert L. Heilbroner, **Business Civilization in Decline,** (New York: W.W. Norton and Company, Inc., 1976) p. 108.

16. "Foundation Reprint No. 7," op. cit., pp. 4-6.

17. Heilbroner, op. cit., pp. 102-103.

18. Bryson, op. cit., p. 12.

APPENDIX

1. Francis A. Shaeffer, **The God Who Is There,** (Downers Grove, Illinois: Inter-Variety Press, 1968), p. 16.

2. Frederick Nymeyer, **Minimal Religion,** (South Holland, Illinois: Libertanian Press, 1964), p. 11.

3. Ibid.

4. Col. R.B. Thieme, Jr., "Bible Study Lectures," Berachah Church, 5139 W. Alabama, Houston, Texas 77027, 1967-1977.

5. John Warwick Montgomery, **Where Is History Going?,** (Grand Rapids: Zondervan Publishing House, 1969), p. 63.

6. Gary North, Editor, Rousas John Rushdoony, "The Quest for Common Ground," **Foundations of Christian Scholarship,** (Vallecito, California: Ross House Books, 1976), p. 35, quoting Cornelius Van Til, **A Letter on Common Grace,** p. 61.

7. Shaeffer, op. cit., p. 17.

8. Proverbs 6:16.

9. Gary North, Editor, C. Gregg Singer, "The Problem of Historical Interpretation," **Foundations of Christian Scholarship,** op. cit., p. 66.

10. Shaeffer, op. cit., p. 47.

11. Gary North, Editor, Frederic N. Andre and Rousas John Rushdoony, "The Adversary Concept," **The Journal of Christian Reconstruction,** Vol. II, No. 2, (Winter, 1975), p. 32, P.O. Box 158, Vallecito, California 95251.

12. North, William N. Blake, "Van Til's Vision for Education," **Foundations of Christian Scholarship,** op. cit., p. 111.

13. "Tomorrow," **U.S. News and World Report,** September 5, 1977, p. 10.

14. John P. DeCecco and Arlene K. Richards, "Civil War In the High Schools: A Way Out of Anarchy," **Psychology Today,** Vol. 9, No. 6, (November, 1975), pp. 51-56.

214

15. "America's Youth: Angry . · .Bored . . . Or Just Confused?," **U.S. News and World Report,** July 18, 1977, p. 18.

16. Ibid.

17. North, Blake, op. cit., pp. 112-113.

18. Ibid., p. 108.

19. Shaeffer, op. cit., p. 19.

20. Irving Kristol, "On the Unfairness of Life," **The Wall Street Journal,** August 16, 1977, Editorial Page.

21. Ibid.

22. Ibid.

23. Ibid.

24. Lawrence Dennis, **The Dynamics of War and Revolution,** (The United States of America: The Weekly Foreign Letter, 1940), p. 125.

25. James C. Patrick, "What the Bible Says About Big Government," **The Freeman,** Vol. 26, No. 3, (March 1976), pp. 176-177.

26. Nymeyer, op. cit., p. 109.

27. Ibid., pp. 109-110.

28. Patrick, op. cit., p. 181.

29. Dennis, op. cit., pp. 36-45.

30. Ibid.

31. North, Lawrence D. Pratt, "The Politics of Pragmatism: Threat to Freedom," **Foundation of Christian Scholarship,** op, cit., pp. 119-125.

32. Kristol, op. cit.

33. Stuart Barton Babbage, **The Vacuum of Unbelief,** (Grand Rapids, Michigan: Zondervan Publishing House, 1969), p. 15.

34. Peter Berger, "The Link Between Capitalism and Democracy," **The Wall Street Journal,** August 1, 1977, Editorial Page.

35. Clarence B. Carson, "World in the Grip of An Idea," **The Freeman,** Vol. 27, No. 2, (February 1977), pp. 100-101.

36. North, Rousas John Rushdoony, "Biblical Law and Western

Civilization," **The Journal of Christian Reconstruction,** op. cit., p. 11.

37. Rev. Rousas John Rushdoony, **Chalcedon Report,** No. 141, (May 1977), p. 1, Chalcedon, P.O. Box 158, Vallecito, California 95251.

38. Ibid.

39. Rev. Rousas John Rushdoony, **Chalcedon Report,** No. 142, (June, 1977), p. 1.

40. North, Rushdoony, "Biblical Law and Western Civilization," op. cit., p. 5.

41. Ibid.

42. Ibid., p. 10.

43. Ibid., p. 12.

44. Ibid., p. 13.

45. Nymeyer, op. cit., p. 106.

46. Kristol, op. cit.

47. Ralf Dahrendorf, "Is Britain Really That Sick," **The Wall Street Journal,** August 18, 1977, Editorial Page.

48. North, Andre and Rushdoony, op. cit., p. 32.

49. Ibid., pp. 29-30.

50. Ibid., p. 32.

51. Rev. Rousas John Rushdoony, **Chalcedon Report,** No. 146, (October, 1977), p. 1.

52. Ibid.

53. Patrick, op. cit., p. 176, quoting Russell Kirk, **The Conservative Mind;** Chicago, Illinois: Henry Requery Company, 1960, p. 482.

54. Patrick, op. cit., p. 176.

55. Clarence B. Carson, "World in the Grip of an Idea," **The Freeman,** Vol. 27, No. 3, (March 1977), p. 180.

56. Nymeyer, op. cit., p. 78.

57. Ibid., p. 103.

58. Matthew 6:19-21.

59. Matthew 6:33.

60. I Timothy 6:10.

61. I Timothy 6:9.

62. Matthew 19:24.

63. Matthew 5:40-42.

64. Matthew 19:21.

65. Acts 20-35.

66. Romans 13:8.

67. Hans F. Sennholz, "The Great Depression," **The Freeman,** Vol. 25, No. 4, (April, 1975), p. 215.

68. Dr. E.F. Schumacher, "The Plowboy Interview," **The Mother Earth News,** No. 42, (November, 1976), p. 13.

69. Ibid., p. 16.

70. Ibid., p. 17.

71. Ibid., p. 16.

72. Heilbroner, op. cit., pp. 112-116.

73. Ibid., p. 122.

74. Ibid., p. 119.

75. "Russian Private Enterprise," **Daily News Digest,** Vol. 4, No. 2, (October 19, 1977), p. 6, quoting **Phoenix Gazette,** October 13, 1977, p. A-6.

76. Clarence B. Carson, "World in the Grip of an Idea," **The Freeman,** Vol. 27, No. 3, (March 1977), p. 171.

77. Riencourt, op. cit., pp. 295-296, quoting Alexis de Tocqueville.

78. Rees-Mogg, op. cit., pp. 21-22.

79. Babbage, op. cit., p. 14.

80. Kenneth O. Gangel, "Arnold Toynbee: The Man and His Message," **Bibliotheca Sacra,** Vol. 134, No. 533, (January-March, 1977), p. 58.

81. Kenneth O. Gangel, "Arnold Toynbee: An Evangelical Evaluation," **Bibliotheca Sacra,** Vol. 134, No. 534, (April-June 1977), p. 153.

82. Ibid., p. 155.

83. "Books," **Psychology Today,** (November, 1975), pp. 18-20.

84. Riencourt, op. cit., pp. 286-287.

85. Ibid., p. 346.

86. Rev. Rousas John Rushdoony, **"Chalcedon Report,"** No. 145, (September, 1977), p. 1.

87. John 8:32.

88. I Samuel 15:3.

89. I Samuel 15:9.

90. I Samuel 31.

91. Rees-Mogg, op. cit., p. 25.

92. Peterson, op. cit., p. 100.

93. "Gann Manuscripts," Lambert Gann Publishing Company, op. cit.

94. Proverbs 23:7.

95. Modin, op. cit., pp. 150-151.